DISCARDED

SH*of*OWERS SPARKS

— *Memories of Encounters with the Love of God* —

STODDARD B. WILLIAMS

ARCHWAY
PUBLISHING

Archway Publishing books may be ordered through booksellers or by contacting:

Archway Publishing
1663 Liberty Drive
Bloomington, IN 47403
www.archwaypublishing.com
1 (888) 242-5904

Because of the dynamic nature of the Internet, any web addresses or
links contained in this book may have changed since publication and
may no longer be valid. The views expressed in this work are solely those
of the author and do not necessarily reflect the views of the publisher,
and the publisher hereby disclaims any responsibility for them.

Any people depicted in stock imagery provided by Getty Images are
models, and such images are being used for illustrative purposes only.
Certain stock imagery © Getty Images.

ISBN: 978-1-4808-8654-4 (sc)
ISBN: 978-1-4808-8655-1 (e)

Library of Congress Control Number: 2019920826

Print information available on the last page.

Archway Publishing rev. date: 01/02/2020

CONTENTS

SHOWERS OF SPARKS

The storyteller, in the bonfire's glow,
from ancient memories filled with tribal lore,
repeats the lessons learned from long ago
and speaks of heroes gone and times before.
Sage words passed down from age to age, like fire,
burn bright to warm the hearts of those who hear,
shedding such light as mind and soul require
to catch the heat of flames no longer near.
The storyteller and the tale are one,
their ageless voices echoing the past,
span time and space with every story spun,
and help to join the first words with the last.
The storyteller stirs the fire and marks
the darkest hours with radiant showers of sparks.

STORYTELLING

When I was a young lad of eight and had a nickel, I would ride my bike into town to Douglas's Homemade Ice Cream Parlor to spend it on one of Mr. Douglas's many-flavored triangular cones. On my way to the store, I would take a quick look behind me to spot any cars heading in the direction in which I was heading, hopefully one that was just about to overtake me. Waiting until it was close enough to make for a tight race, I would, with a sudden burst of energy and frantic pedaling, race it to the next telephone pole. This, I thought, was a great sport of my own invention. It was and it wasn't.

One day, while riding into town with a cousin of mine, I shared this racing innovation with him. His lackluster response was, "So? I do that all the time!" In that moment, a glint of new understanding flashed in my young brain. This new truth, as simple as it seems, was very significant for me at that time. It joined me to rest of the world in which I lived. I understood that I was very much like others, and others were very much like me. What I had judged to be unique and singular was, in one way or another, shared by others. I have more to join me with others in our common experiences than I will ever find in my isolated theories and opinions. The reality was that someone else might well have used their bike as I used mine, raced as I raced, or something very like it. We, and others, are more alike than we know.

Stories are rare coins, earned through the hard work of living, valuable only as they are exchanged, only as they are shared. That is why our stories of the profound in the simple, of the extraordinary in the ordinary, of the amazing in the familiar, are so important. Our shared humanity is affirmed in our stories, and we are already connected with one another by the older stories from which our stories spring, by the showers of sparks that ignite our fires.

For me, such stories bridge the spaces that can so easily separate us, such spaces as time and place and relationships. Stories, factual or fictional, become personal expressions of our doubts and beliefs, our convictions and confusions, our hopes and our fears. Our stories become a way we can join hands with those who travel with us now, with those who are no longer with us, and with those who are not yet with us. Stories remind us of who we are as individuals while they join us with the larger story of family, community, and humanity.

Stories are like precious moments of life, captured on the film of memory, stored in the attics of our daily living, enabling us to reenter places and events no longer accessible in any other way. Every once in a while, such precious artifacts need to be taken down from their storage bins—some very personal, some communal—into the living room of the present to be viewed from that new perspective. In that light, they can be relived, renewed, and reevaluated. Often it is in viewing them over again that we will discover inspiration, confirmation, new appreciation, and additional meaning for our lives. We are able to reconnect once again with a face long gone, an experience dimmed by distance, an act of kindness forgotten, sparks that have been lost to the winds of time and normalcy, viewed once again.

One time, while going through a trunk of my dad's memorabilia, I found a small cigar box filled with old films he had taken years and years ago. The films were developed but had not been made into pictures. The film was still in small, individual canisters, and, when I pulled the film out of the holder and viewed it against a strong light, the past was once again visible to me.

ON VIEWING OLD FILM

I knew the film was still there
in the limbo of neglect
since it had been created
years ago.
                              I am on it,
in it,
a young boy,
Timeless,
preserved on celluloid,
a brittle roll of combustible negatives
seen in the light of nostalgia.
I view it again
one frame at a time:
sparkling moments,
precious people,
brief glimpses of life resurrections in black and white
colored by memories enhanced by experience,
valued by love

I have written these stories and poems as I have reviewed the filmlike memories of my own life. My stories are colored by recollection, enhanced by experience, and valued by love. I write to share my showers of sparks with others, believing that there are those who might enjoy them as I have. I write to bring the past into the present with some of what life has shared with me. In the telling of these stories, I have made no attempt to be socially relevant or morally profound. What I have attempted to do is to recall and retell some of those special times when the showers of sparks generated by my personal experiences have fallen on me.

These sparks are not sorted by theme, nor do they have any specific lessons to teach. They are simply retold as they are remembered, as they witness to me of the wonder of being alive, of living in the love of God. These stories are about dancing movements of grace, significant moments that still sparkle and shine for me with a special glow. They are expressions of that mystery that is constantly tugging at my heart, inspiring my soul, and lifting my spirit.

By their very nature, sparks are momentary and unpredictable, quickly fading from sight, leaving only the afterglow of their brilliance. They come as if by accident, carried by unpredictable and unexpected winds. I have been touched, even singed, by their showers. Like Moses before the burning bush, I am led to bow down in reverential awe before the splendor of their presence.

REMEMBERED

The intensity of intimacy
The desire for intensity
The inability to act as desired
The ability to act as requested
The excitement of living
The dread of dying
The love of mother
The loss of father
Twirling on a tire swing
Feeding dogs
Riding bikes
Swimming in the pond
Jumping in the hay,
Sneaking out at midnight
An aircraft hangar with my father,
A living room without my father
The smell of spring

The sound of sleigh bells and firecrackers
The feel of grass
Tears of pain and sorrow
Happy laughter
Cousins playing
The Shadow and Jack Benny
Marbles and roller skates
Hunting snapping turtles
War, blackouts,
National Geographic Magazine.
Hot summer afternoon board games
Cold winter mornings on the grate
Old cars traveling to the moon,
Woodpile sailing ships
Driving a carriage into disaster,
Friends long gone

WHY REFLECTIONS?

As part of my storytelling, I will share some of my reflections on each story. These reflections will include what, to me, are insights and discoveries and conclusions that seem important to me because of the events and experiences the stories recount.

Reflecting on particular experiences is a very important part of living. Reflecting often uncovers treasures that otherwise would be overlooked and neglected. When life is happening, it seldom gives us time to evaluate or appreciate its subtle depths, its finer nuances, its grander meanings. Perhaps readers will also reflect upon these stories and find treasures for themselves. I surely hope so.

SECOND HEARING

I wrote a poem
and later learned
its meaning.
The words,
when future read,
spoke new truths,
revealed
heights and depths
not understood
when first I wrote them,
revealing more
than I had intended.

SPARK #1

THE INFLEXIBLE FLYER

It is only now, seven decades later, that I can remember with fondness the Christmas of 1942. It was not so when I was twelve years old. That particular Christmas seemed to me a complete disaster and a huge disappointment. My father had been dead for a few months, and I was not healed. My mom, a young widow who had left school in the tenth grade to go to work to help provide for her family, was still working as a bank teller to provide for my sister and for me.

We—my mother, my sister, and I—were living at the home of my deceased father's mother. Her house was a very large, brown brick, three-story, mansion of a home that had, at one time, been host to senators, governors, garden parties, and church picnics. It still gave testimony to crumbling affluence and declining influence, an honorable lineage and noteworthy heritage, but the grand times were over.

Since Black Tuesday family members—aunts, uncles, and cousins—were also living at "Nana's house" and had been there before our family moved in, mostly for financial reasons. Times were hard, the Second World War was on, and we were not as wealthy as the home we lived in or the name we lived under might lead outsiders to conclude.

Being the last family to move into Nana's house, we lived where there was room. That happened to be on the third floor, a hard climb but nice living space, two bedrooms and a bath. The house smelled of lavender soap, success, old age, prestige, and difficult questions about who we were and who we were supposed to be.

On cold days, steam from the coal furnace would bang upward to the window-seat radiators in our rooms. I would often curl up on one of these heated seats and stare out the window, the ragged remnants of a clay tennis court and the slimy green water of a shallow ice pond showing their desperate need for maintenance. Hooked to an unused greenhouse was a one-car garage where an uncle's Chevrolet found refuge. Further on, I could see the impressive main barn with its outbuildings and its huge, two-story hay doors standing open to the weather. Not long ago, a pig, split in half, had been hung by block and tackle from one of those doors.

In one of the back rooms of the barn, behind the former living quarters for a hired hand, the remnants of my dad's short life were stored in old, black leather trunks. All that remained of his life, his trophies, and his personal belongings—was consigned to that sad, remote, and tragic space. It was a place I often visited alone to grieve, to wonder, and to cope.

Snow was in the air, and Christmas was just one day away. *Tonight is Christmas Eve. We'll be going to Uncle Sam's for the family Christmas party,* I thought without joy. *Santa will be there like every other year, even though we all know that someone will be playing the part. Probably Uncle Jim. He tries hard, but he doesn't fool anyone. Anyway, it might be fun.* Then I began to think about Christmas morning and what I might find under the tree. "Don't expect very much," my mother had told me several times. "The war has made gifts scarce and expensive." I knew my mom had very little money to spend on Christmas presents. I also knew that I wanted a new sled.

*Everyone slides down the hill at Uncle Sam's—*so my sad thinking went. *Not only do my cousins do it, but all of the kids in the neighborhood do it too. Everyone but me. All I have is that huge sled Dad built for me before he died.* That was a fact. The only sled I did have was a great hulk of a machine built by my father when I was eight. It was both a sled and a cart, meant to have wheels in the summer, and runners in the winter. It was so heavy and cumbersome that I could barely move it, much less pull it up a hill. It looked wonderful. The idea of it was grand, but it just never did work right. It was impressive to look at but just awful to use. It, like the house in which we now lived, was not what it seemed. Besides, you could not do a "belly-flopper" on it.

Many things that look good from the outside, that seem like they ought to be good, just fail to deliver. I felt that surely this Christmas would also fail because I wanted the impossible: a different, better, lighter, and faster sled. A Flexible Flyer. I wanted to be able to join my friends in sledding without being laughed at or left behind. I wanted to be able to take a running start and belly-flop with the rest of the kids on the hill.

Everything was lined up against that happening. The war was real; the armed forces needed metal to fight the Germans and the Japanese. My mom had no money to buy such an expensive gift, and no one really knew what I wanted anyway. On top of that, there were no Flexible Flyers to be had. I was selfish to want so much. I needed to be content with whatever I got, whatever that might be. So, even before I received anything, I knew I would be disappointed.

I turned against those feelings. I would tell myself that it was Jesus's birthday and not mine. With those thoughts, I slowly slipped into a sad and lonely sleep, wishing my dad were there, hoping against hope for a Christmas where dreams would come true, feeling guilty that I didn't like my father's sled.

The Christmas party at Uncle Sam's turned out to be just what I had expected. Santa arrived with sleigh bells and the sound of reindeer landing on the roof, with candy canes and hard candy in little boxes. The adults all seemed to be truly enjoying themselves, speaking of things about which I knew nothing: business, war, men in the service, and politics.

I sat with a cousin on the landing of a great staircase, high above the family's happy festivities, sucking on pieces of hard Christmas candy. It was the proper place to think dark thoughts of disappointments, failures, and heavy loads. I just wanted to be home so that tomorrow would come and I could move past my sadness and loneliness.

My sister seemed to be having a good time with her friends. My mother seemed just fine and full of happy thoughts. In my unhappy frame of mind, none of that mattered. Santa's laugh sounded fake, and his jolly attitude seemed forced and foolish. No one asked me how I was doing nor even seemed to care. That was fine with me. We seemed to stay forever. I did not say "Good night" or "Thank you" when we finally left for home.

Christmas morning, it snowed. That would be just wonderful for those fortunate enough to receive skis or skates or sleds for Christmas. I curled up on the window seat and looked out of my third-floor window at a world growing ever whiter. Someone had closed the barn doors on the weather, and the slimy green pond water was covered with a clean, thin layer of ice. *If this keeps up, someone could shovel the snow off of the ice so people could skate on the pond. That would be fun for them,* I thought.

I got dressed in my Sunday clothes and went down to the dining room to have my breakfast. I was not hungry. Everyone seemed to be excited—everyone but me. After breakfast, the whole family waited for the doors to the living room to be opened by our Nana. This was the place where the Christmas tree and all the presents were kept.

In spite of myself, I was becoming excited. *What had my mom found to give me?* I wondered. Was it possible that she had found a Flexible Flyer? I just knew she had not. The doors opened, and we all rushed in with many expressions of joy and expectation.

There, behind a Christmas tree, leaning against the wall, I saw a sled, bigger than a Flexible Flyer, with a different kind of steering, and with round runners instead of flat ones. *Mom has found a sled for me,* I observed, my excitement turning to disappointment. The sled had a red ribbon tied on it. Mom glowed with pride and love as she led me to it. "Here is the sled you were hoping for," she said. I had said "Flexible Flyer," and she had heard "sled." "I had to look just everywhere for it," she continued. "I finally found this one in a little shop near the bank. I hope you like it. The salesman said it would go faster than any other sled on the market today."

That's because there are no Flexible Flyers on the market today, I thought. Just looking at that heavy, ungainly, round-runner sled, I knew she had been sold a bill of goods. It was obvious that those round runners would quickly sink right through the snow to bare ground. The metal was already rusting and bending. I put the sled on the floor and lay on it, trying to steer it. The sled just would not steer properly nor turn sharply enough, no matter how hard I tried. It would not easily avoid trees or people. It was not a Flexible Flyer.

My disappointment must have shown because Mom repeated again how the war effort had made things difficult to find, how she had looked and looked for a Flexible Flyer but just could not find one, and how this was the very best she could do. I held onto the rope that was hooked to the steering bar and smiled and thanked her for all her efforts, but I failed to thank her for the sled. My heart was sad. I feared this sled was a confirmation that what looked fine seldom worked out in my life.

In that mood, I reasoned that the new sled would be too heavy. I knew I was not strong enough to handle its bulk. Instead, it would be an embarrassment to me. I would have to struggle up the hill behind everyone else, just as it happened with the monster sled my dad had built for me. With poor steering and round runners, this new sled would be the slowest sled, both coming up and sliding down the hill. In addition, it did not lend itself to belly-floppers, a slider's most impressive maneuver to pick up speed and slide further. Dad's mistake was still to be my disappointment, if with another sled.

All my expectations proved valid when, on my first trip up that troublesome hill, I was last in line, and on my first effort at a belly-flopper, the sled sank right to the bare ground and stopped short, catapulting me forward into the ice-crusted snow onto my cold, red face, bloody from a cut lip.

That is the way the Christmas of 1942 ended, with sadness and disappointment. Joy was not in the Inflexible Flyer.

REFLECTIONS ON "THE INFLEXIBLE FLYER"

You might find this story a sad one. That would be one response, but not the only one. It is only in later life that I have come to see the true spark that glowed for me in that Christmas gift. Now, as I remember that Christmas, I see that my sadness and disappointment were more about grieving for my father than about the poor characteristics of a sled. I also see my mom in a different light. As I move my eyes from my father's poor choice of a sled for me to my mother's poor choice of a sled for me, I can now see her deep love, not her poor choice of a gift. She knew she would be forced to provide less than I wanted. She knew she could only do what she could do, give what she could give, and offer what she had to offer. She could not be my father, provide for my every desire, and take care of my every whim. She was a widow, as alone in her ways as I was in mine, and with very limited resources with which to care for my sister and for me. Mom was doing her best to provide for our needs. She could only love me the best way she knew with what she had and trust that somehow, someday, I would understand.

It has taken way too long for me to acknowledge my mother's love as it was shown in that substitute for a Flexible Flyer. It has taken even longer to understand the love in my father's gift. Self-centeredness so easily hides the sparks of love. Just as that sad Christmas disappointed me then, it now it fills me with real joy. If, at that time, I saw only the gift I did not receive, now I see the precious gift that I did receive. As far from the mark as the gift seemed to fall when I received it, love now shines in that Inflexible Non-Flyer and in the one who gave it. She loved me the very best way she knew and as fully as she was able. My own personal needs and desires hid that love from my heart. Now I know. The prize was not in the gift, but in the giver. As I remember these things, I think of all the other times I may have missed love's spark because of my own preoccupations, expectations, desires, and unmet needs.

I will say now what I did not say then: Thank you, Mom, for the gift of your love. In spite of your own needs, you searched for a gift that might please me, and though you had little for yourself, you spent precious treasure on me. You understood me and loved me even when I was unthankful. Thank you, Mom.

The sled that I could not carry now carries me. Those rusty, round runners sinking into the snow now fly me down the hills of Christmas on wings of love.

As I remembered and reevaluated that Christmas, I was reminded of a poem I wrote when I was about fourteen years old. It seemed a nice thought then but has acquired more depth as I have acquired more years. The question is this: Do we recognize Divine Sparks? Are we thankful for them even when they are gone?

THE QUESTION

If all the things
that we have loved
were but to last one day,

would we protest their vanishing
or weep the time away?
Or would we spend the last short hours
in thanking God above
that we have had the privilege
of having things to love?

SPARK #2

A VERY SPECIAL GIFT

orn into a troubled marriage and leaving tenth grade to go to
work to help support the rest of her family, my mother was,
from her earliest years, a very special gift. She was a person who
gave herself, her love, her interest, and her service unselfishly to
others.

Along with most other women of her age, mother led a
memorable life that spanned great changes in both technology
and culture. Her life began in a world in which she went to school
in a sleigh in winter and in a buggy the rest of the year and each
morning had the task of cleaning the glass chimneys of the oil
lamps used for light the night before. She washed her clothes in a
tub using a scrub board. She put cardboard in her shoes to keep
the dirt and wet from coming through the holes in their bottoms.

Her life moved on to a world in which she sewed the canvas on
the wings and fuselage of the low-winged monoplane her husband
designed and built. She helped paint it with dope and then saw it
fly, the first such aircraft ever build in the United States.

Her life moved her on from her midwest upbringing to the
world of her husband's family in a New England atmosphere of
ancestry, affluence, and influence. She entered that world as a
widow in a strange land. As a widow, she took care of her brother,
his children, her sister, her sister's children, her mother, her
own children, and the neighbors' kids as need arose. When she

remarried, she gave the same love to her new husband's children as she gave to her own.

To illustrate the kind of sparks that issued from her life, I will mention but two. The first has to do with her car.

When her second husband died, she took over his Buick, a big, black, luxurious, well-equipped sedan. She treasured that car for the freedom and comfort it provided her. I will confess that I was a bit envious of that car. It was years newer and far more upscale than mine. So it was with a sense of guilty joy that I received from her to me the gift of that Buick. I had come to visit with her at her condo one Saturday afternoon. When we had settled ourselves in the living room, she simply handed me the keys to the Buick and told me that she was giving up driving. She explained that she could no longer see the road well enough to drive safely, so she would drive no more.

Wow! What a relief not to have to make that call for her, not to have to take the keys away from her, or worse, see the car wrecked or she or someone else injured. And I got the car, which I drove for several years, enjoying it greatly. But her real gift to me was not the car but her courageous attitude, giving up her freedom on behalf of the safety of others. That was a bright and welcome spark.

This was her way of life, a way of grace which took what life offered her, good or less than good, happy or not so happy, and made it all a blessing. When life was prosperous and full of possibilities she use those resources to help, encourage and up build others. When life diminished her financially and physically, she used her attitude and her wisdom to bless others. Never did she argue or blame or complain. It was not in her nature. Bright sparks of love in all conditions was her way.

My second example has to do with the time she decided to enter herself into the Masonic Home for continued care. It meant spending down her last few dollars to go on Medicare. Still, it seemed to be what she wanted.

My wife and I had opened our home to her when she could no longer be by herself. We gave her a bedroom, a living room, and a bath. Still, we could not give her the attention she needed. I had a church to supervise, and my wife worked at the child care center at the church. These duties took both of us out of the house for the best part of the day.

One morning at breakfast, my mother asked us into her living room for a talk. She told us that our home, as loving as it was, did not provide her with enough interaction for her to feel comfortable. She shared this fact with us without blame, rancor, or anger. It was simply a fact. She was going to spend down her remaining funds and move to the Masonic Home. Another *wow*. What we, in the very near future, might have been forced to do, she did with a willing heart.

The day before she was scheduled to leave, she told me she had prayed to God to give her a mission for her life in her new Masonic home. My wife and I were excited to know what it might be. She was happy to tell us that the mission she believed she had been given was very simple and yet very demanding. She was to make the people around her smile. So simple. So profound. So like her.

It was no surprise that the nurses and attendants at the Masonic Home loved her. She accomplished her mission over and over again. They would give her a roommate who was unhappy and unpleasant and, in few months, she would have that person smiling. In some cases, that was a major accomplishment and reflected the fact that she was nonjudgmental and a wonderful listener. Her love was always unconditional. It is no wonder that her children and grandchildren and great-grandchildren call her blessed and remember her with appreciation and delight.

REFLECTIONS ON "A VERY SPECIAL GIFT"

With the advantage of hindsight, I confess that I was more grateful for the gift of the Buick than I was for the gift of her ability to give up a piece of that freedom for the benefit of others, a gift that freed me from a most onerous task. Good lives lived for others send the sparks of selfless living into the future.

In addition, I was more relieved at having the responsibility of caring for her lifted from my shoulders then I was for the gracious and non-blaming spirit in which she went about doing it.

It is fitting that she loved roses and Queen Ann's lace. It is more than a coincidence that these very things summed up her life. Roses speak of beauty, and Queen Ann's lace speaks of grace. The showers of sparks given off by her life were full of beauty and grace. At her passing, I wrote the following poem.

ROSES AND LACE

She's always moved
with easy grace
from room to room
to make each place
most welcoming
with rose and lace.
When circumstance
forced her to close
her spacious rooms,
her spirit chose
to fill the rest
with lace and rose.
Time after time,
her rooms decreased;

yet, as doors shut,
she's never ceased
with rose and lace
to bless the least.
When one small room
was her embrace,
her hopeful words
and smiling face
filled it still
with rose and lace.
But such a room
must also close
when it no longer
can enclose
her vast expense
of lace and rose,
so she will rise
as Jesus rose
to many rooms
that will disclose
a heaven filled
with lace and rose.

SPARK #3

THE BARN

Some of my favorite childhood memories center on the summer months, when eight or ten of the family cousins came together at our grandparents' farm. The games we invented or employed to entertain ourselves come to life again as I am remembering them.

By mutual consent and for common enjoyment, we used the barn next to the house, along with the chicken yard attached to the barn, as our playground. The five acres that went with the house and barn became the canvas on which we acted out our fancies.

The barn was huge and had intriguing passages, hiding places, haylofts, grain bins, an insulated room where ice could be stored, and a cold cellar where apples, potatoes, and other vegetables could be kept over the winter. This barn also sheltered many interesting treasures. Among them, we valued sleighs, buggies, an ancient car, and outbuildings chock full of farm implements, machinery, and all sorts of interesting items. None of these treasures were placed off limits to us. They became part of our make-believe world of adventure.

An example: trees blown down by the 1938 hurricane had been sawed into logs and piled up behind the barn between three tall pines that had escaped such destruction. This pile formed a platform six feet wide and twenty feet long. This woodpile platform became our sailing ship, the three pines became our three masts, and the top of the woodpile became the deck from which we sailed the seven seas. We could climb these masts and keep watch over the ocean for enemy ships and for people who needed our help. We sailed our ship as pirates, as the Royal Navy, as Spanish explorers, and as a Coast Guard vessel. Along the way, we caught hundreds of bad people, sank hundreds of ships, and helped many in distress.

Another example: the old car in the barn also became a vehicle for imagined trips to faraway lands and exciting destinations. We would travel across the country, go to the moon, or, like Buck Rogers, travel to the stars. The car offered us complicated gauges and gear shifts, leather seats, levers to push or pull, and a huge, non-working motor to feed our imaginations and support our games. Better than a McDonald's playroom any day.

We were serious about our fun. Hide-and-seek was a popular game, happening throughout the whole barn and taking up hours of search and find. There were no places that were off limits, even though the places to hide were many and difficult to discover. We did not mind the difficulty. Once, when hiding in a grain bin, I waited over an hour to be found. Waiting to be discovered was not pleasant or easy, but it was great fun. The only things that could end a game were food or injury. The unspoken rules were never to give up and to stay in the game until it was over.

Many of the games we played took place at one end of the barn in a chicken yard. That yard was in the middle of a ring of outbuildings attached to the barn. We created a western town in that special space. The town had a jail, a bank, a barbershop, a blacksmith shop, a gun shop, and a grocery. In this make-believe town, we could rob a bank, hunt for the robbers, jail crooks, escape from jail, shoot it out with bad guys, become our heroes, and act in heroic roles. In this town, we could sharpen our swords and have swordfights, oil our guns and have gunfights, hold court and have lawyer fights, get our capes and have bullfights.

The wonder of it all is that each of us assumed the role given to us by the rest. Even when violence was central to our game, the basis of the game was peaceful, resting on cooperation between us. No one was left out. No one was belittled. No one was ignored. If we were killed, we were given a new part to play. We shared the game together.

One summer, the oldest cousin in our little group decided that the youngest cousins should be the subjects of a wedding. The youngest girl cousin would be the bride. The next-to-youngest boy cousin, myself, would be the groom. She and I agreed, excited to have center stage for a brief moment. The group went to work planning the whole affair. They found clothing for us, fancy hats and grown-up coats, all very special. From the kitchen, they solicited refreshment for after the ceremony. They gathered flowers for a bouquet for her and a boutonniere for me. They even located a Bible for the preacher, the one who conceived the whole idea. He would hold it when he conducted the ceremony. I have a photograph of the couple, all dressed up and happy as can be.

It is still a wonderful memory. After we had all grown up and moved past such games, the bride's real husband would introduce me to his friends as his wife's first husband. Special memories made by children at play.

REFLECTIONS ON "THE BARN"

The games we enjoyed as children are not repeatable in the world of today. Electronic computers have replaced the barn with spaces and games where such imagination is no longer required. But the role-playing we enjoyed as children, the freedom to do so, and the space in which to act out our visions and aspirations provided us with showers of sparks that electronics cannot produce or provide. These sparks were shared by all of us. Each of us had our part in their sparkle, and all of us benefited from their light. They were part of the fire that turned vision into fact, idea into actuality, games into life fulfilling experiences of cooperation and loving acceptance.

It seems to me that our expressions of imagination are an important part of our faith. They enable us to envision the stories of faith, the people of faith, the spaces where faith operates, the hope that faith gives to us about the yet-to-be in the face of what is. They open possibility and confirm promises. They enable us to see God and speak with the Holy Spirit. They put us in touch with our souls. Their absence may account for the lack of faith among so many in today's world.

All this from a barn that is now an apartment house, a chicken yard (our western town) that no longer exists, an old car (the vehicle that provided us with rides to the moon) turned into scrap, a woodpile (a ship for sailing the seven seas) long since reduced to dust, and the imagination of children. What a gift to each of us who were blessed to play together. The showers of sparks our play engendered enlighten and delight us to this very day.

These sparks reignite our lives at surprising times and in unsuspected ways. That is the subject of the following poem.

A CHILD'S IMAGINATION

Is timeless,
wins every fight,
saves every prisoner,
defeats every enemy,
rules every kingdom
controls every situation
sees heaven,
knows God,

visits the future
and the past
with what is at hand,
        knocks on other dimensions,
        accomplishes any task,
        becomes any hero.

SPARK #4
A LEAP OF FAITH

It was the summer of 1943. I was thirteen years old and in the clutches of a strong desire to break free of the routine, to discover a new, more appealing, and more exciting life. That desire was pushing me to do things that were different and daring. This pent-up need for actual adventure had a headlock on my attitude and wouldn't let me go. It had gained a nifty half nelson on me, and, it seemed to me, the only way to break its grip was to improve the boring sameness of my life.

This began to happen on a Sunday when my Mom, my sister, and I had gone to visit some old family friends for what promised to be another uneventful and tedious afternoon. These friends lived out in the country, away from the usual and the normal and the predictable. On what seemed to me to be their vast estate, there was a barn with a small guest apartment. I sensed that this apartment could be the perfect place to undo the half nelson that boredom had placed round my life. Could I contrive a quick move toward an adventure in a new setting?

So it was that I asked my mom if I could spend some time in that barn apartment with a cousin. Perhaps a weekend would do. Would she, I pleaded, ask her friends for permission? No, she would not. But she would allow me to ask. So I took up the challenge and asked permission. The owners told me that they would be away most of the summer, but that I had their permission to spend a

Friday and Saturday night in the guesthouse. If I wished to bring along a friend, I could. We would have to cook for ourselves and clean up after ourselves. Other than that, everything was fine. Sounded great to me.

So it was that I asked my friend Bobby to share my adventure. He did not know where we were going, but he saw the possibilities of an exciting weekend with the same level of enthusiasm I enjoyed. We were ready and eager to go. It was going to be a great escapade.

I figured that we would just grab the few things we would need and then just go; what these specific things might be, I didn't know nor care. Adventures can't be planned; they just need to happen. Bobby, and his mom, proved more practical, knowing that planning would add considerable comfort and pleasure to our experience. At Bobby's suggestion, therefore, we planned a menu and tried to identify some of the things we wanted to do on our weekend, things like exploring the countryside, listening to the radio, playing cards, and reading Superman and Batman comics.

The Thursday before we were to go, we shopped for our groceries: corn flakes, peanut butter, jelly, bread, milk, canned spaghetti, soda, cookies, hamburger, orange juice, and comic books. The adventure began.

The weekend we had chosen for our adventure proved to start with a soggy, damp, and dreary, un-summerlike day. It was late on a cool, rainy Friday afternoon that my mother drove Bobby and me to our adventure in the pouring rain. We could, she said, fend for ourselves. Reality can be cold and foreboding, and an adventure can be very uncomfortable. But for the two of us, it was exciting, even though it was difficult.

We hauled our damp sleeping bags, food, cards, radio, and clothing into the chill, clammy, empty, lifeless, sterile apartment that was to be our base camp. The lamps and ceiling lights had small, low-wattage bulbs in them, and turning them on only seemed to add gloom to the already stale, depressing, and tomblike atmosphere of our new quarters. Our adventure, if it were to be a satisfying one, was off to a slow, drizzly beginning. But cold, wet weather could not dampen our adventurous spirits, youth being what it tends to be.

Even though the rain and the lateness of the hour prevented us from going outside to explore the woods, we could read our comic books, eat our cookies, and drape our sleeping bags around our shoulders for warmth. And so we did, even as the late afternoon moved us uneasily toward night. The weather did not improve, the wind picked up, the barn rattled and shook, and night descended upon us all too soon.

If this was to be our grand adventure, it certainly was beginning in a manner we had not envisioned. Still, hope prevailed over circumstance. We heated the spaghetti, sat where we wanted, ate as much as we wanted and drank what we wanted, turned the radio up as loud as we wanted, and pretended we were having a good time. Then we exchanged our comic books, ate more cookies, drank more Pepsi-Colas, and pretended we were having a good time. Then we crawled into our sleeping bags, talked of all the strange and wonderful things we had thought or learned or invented, and pretended we were having a good time. After a time, we grew used to the strange noise all around us, the shadows that flickered about us, the strange bed under us, and the fears we could not name, and we drifted off to light and troubled sleep pretending we were having a good time.

Morning came with disappointing grayness, as dreary as the previous day. No sign of either sun or warmth. But still our spirits would not be dampened. We would not be trapped inside for another day by the wet weather. We would defy the elements. We would have our adventure if it cost us our comfort, our health, our dryness, and our mothers' displeasure. We would sally forth into the wild outdoors, no matter the rain or the chill.

So, having bravely washed up in cold water, having dutifully eaten our corn flakes, milk, and toast with jam, and having faithfully brushed our teeth, we descended the stairs into the wet and cold of our exploit, full of heroic intentions and bold ambitions.

From the bottom step, the tree line at the edge of the lawn beckoned us with turkey cry, wind song, and paths that wandered off like fingers, bidding us come and follow. We obeyed, bounding into the New England wood like hounds on the scent, paying no attention to the damp grass drenching our cuffs or the sharp branches scratching our arms or the mist rising up around us from the wet earth with an eerie whiteness that hid the ground from our view only a few yards in front of our leaping feet.

This was our adventure, our freedom, our vision, and our moment. We were, if only for a few hours, beyond the bounds of the normal, beyond parental control. We were on our own. We flew, we soared, we ran, we shouted, we laughed, we exalted, we examined, we explored, deeper and deeper into the heart of the unknown. I was moving within my joy, rain forgotten, chill ignored, boredom defeated. I dashed and plunged, following my inspired energy, leaping logs, bounding over rocks and ravines, light as air, strong as Atlas, happy as hope. My friend was elsewhere doing his thing. Life exploded within me. It was all beauty and pleasure and freedom. The woods and I rejoiced in each other.

And then it happened, suddenly and abruptly. I had come to an embankment that dropped sharply away from my feet. This was not, I reasoned, an obstacle—it was an opportunity, and I would take it. This sharp decline offered me a launching pad for a gigantic leap, a giant step, a mighty, earth-straddling stride, a brief, ecstatic flight from earth to heaven and back. In pure confidence, I sailed forth from the summit, up and out, pushing off with enthusiasm.

But just here, in the middle of my flight, in the midst of my joy, at the apex of my adventure, I was hauled up short, stopped, flight aborted, joy canceled, trip suspended. I remember it today as if it happened two hours ago. There I was, on my way to a record broad jump, when I was grasped in mid-air by an unseen force. It caught me mid-flight, arrested my forward momentum, stopped me dead in the air, and dropped me straight down onto the ground no more than two feet from where I had started my jump. It was as if I had run into a glass wall. It seemed like someone had erected a barrier I could not pass. A hand had caught hold of my shirt and set me down on the seat of my pants.

But, as unnerving as that experience was, it was not as startling as the roaring noise and the rushing wind that came with the eighteen-wheeled truck that hammered past me, a foot in front of where I had landed. Sitting there bewildered, confused, and frightened, I saw that the space into which I had jumped, the very place where I had been stopped, was no longer woodland. It was the verge of a highway. Had my forward progress not been stopped, I would have ended my jump under the wheels of a gigantic truck.

I sat there for a while just where I had landed, shaking and full of fear, relief, shock, and awe. I had been saved from death by an unseen hand in a miraculous intervention that was miles and miles beyond my understanding. Yet the experience had been real, the jump real, the sudden stop real, the truck real, the possibility of being crushed beneath that truck as real as death.

Here was a spark of considerable brightness. In the pursuit of youthful exploration and adventure, I had experienced the presence of a power that had literally saved my life. In the midst of small hopes and gentle satisfactions, I had received a priceless gift. Along with the little joys I could name, I had received a blessing beyond naming. My adventure had provided me with more than I could ever have imagined or planned. But then, life has seldom been what I planned for. It has always been more.

The more I view the event in the woods from the perspective of a long and blessed life, the more meaning it gathers for me. When it happened, sitting there, next to the road, counting my blessings, I was ever so grateful to be alive. How much more so now, every day being the gift of life to me. I know that life intervened on my behalf that day. That single event has reminded me again and again that my Creator is with me even in my unguarded moments of careless joy.

The sparks that glowed in the woods that day taught me some important lessons. Among them: it is not always jumping ahead that matters, no matter the joy. Sometimes joy needs to be interrupted. Sometimes I need to be brought up short, stopped, and sat down hard before something really bad happens. That is not failure; it is love. I have learned that uncontrolled self-expression can get me into sudden trouble. I have learned not only that are angels real, but that they have the power and authority to act in my life. I have learned that, even though my earthly father (protector) was dead, my heavenly Father, God, was watching over me. I have no reason to feel sorry for that boy in the woods.

REFLECTIONS ON "A LEAP OF FAITH"

Only a very few times since have I known the spontaneous and irrepressible joy I experienced running through those woods with my friend. But I do recall one of those times. I was a young child of seven or eight, on the front lawn of my grandparents' home. Part of their front lawn was a long, sloping grassy hill. On several occasions, I would curl my small body inside one half of a cut-in-two cider barrel and roll down that hill. On that wild and whirling ride, I would be tossed about like clothes spinning in a dryer. When I finally came to a stop, I remember lying on the lawn at the bottom of the hill, dizzy with the spin, open to joy, loving the grass on which I was sprawled.

On reflection, it has been in the simple that I have most often encountered the profound. It has been most often in the ordinary that glory has touched me. It has been my experience that the invisible speaks to me through the visible, and the infinite speaks to me in the present moment. But why not? That is the way we speak to one another, is it not?

GREENING LOVE

In cramped delight
I rode the barrel down
as land and sky
tumbled round
until, in dizzy joy
like circus clown
from funny car,
I spilled out
on the ground.
There, on the lawn,
I lay in disarray
enjoying afterglow
of whirling mind,
as summer melted me
into its giddy day
and clouds formed images
for me to find.
All innocent of ugliness or dark,
I joined things sacred, full of mirth,
the daisy, dandelion, lark,
the soft wind whispering

of beauty's worth.
And you,
my true companion on that hill,
sweet grass, I loved you then,
and always will.

SPARK #5

DREAMS OF LIFE

Issues of death came into my life quite early, while I was still a very young person. Please don't misunderstand me. I'm not only referring to a strong consciousness of my own mortality, as real and frightening as that seemed to me at the time. I am also referring to how, early on, the deaths of some very significant people in my life affected me in a negative way. While maturity may have taught me that the sad and painful experience of losing family or friends to death is not particularly unique, when I was nine and ten and into my teens, death seemed to me to be a private and personal darkness, an interior issue that was mine alone. For me, at that time, death was a fear to be faced and fought by myself, alone, in the deepest parts of my personal life. There, beneath the surface of normalcy, the fear and dread of death cast their frightening shadows, occasionally revealing themselves to me in dreams of quiet terror. Such a dark condition rendered me in need of a spark of light.

This unreasoned fear must have begun about the time my father died. I was nine at the time, and such a loss was more than I could reasonably understand or that with which I could emotionally cope. So it all went underground, grief unexpressed, tears unshed, sadness unspoken, and loss unmeasured. My father's funeral was held in the front parlor of my nana's home, and my mom lifted me up to give my dad a final, goodbye kiss before they closed the coffin lid on him for the last time. My lips met cold, hard flesh that knew me not. It was a fearful experience.

Not too long after my dad died, my nana died. Then my next-door neighbor died, a boy my age with whom I played football and baseball. He fell off a milk truck and was killed. Then my other grandmother, my mother's mother, died. She lived with us and died at home, in her bed. Then my aunt, who lived with us and had multiple Sclerosis, died at our home. Then my uncle, who had lived with us, died. All the while, other, less intimate relations were also dying, as were soldiers in the war. I may not have all these deaths in the correct order, but they were so close together that it makes no difference. For me, death was the order of the day. It seemed to me that death was everywhere and would ruin every good thing that might otherwise happen.

So, in defense, I shut my fear and sadness up in my innermost, private, for-me-only self. I believed that if I were to allow those monstrous dreams to roam about in my thoughts they would destroy my life, darken my sunlight, crush my breath, and devour my joy.

But such fears could and would not be contained. I had neither the resources nor the ability to confine them or control them. With the power of an enemy, they found their way into my dreams. Those dreams were frequent and deeply troubling, and there was one recurring dream that I vividly remember. In it, I am in a graveyard, it is night, and I am given a chair on which I am to sit by the side of my dead aunt. She is in a casket in a grave, and I am there so she won't be alone. As I sit, she slowly decays. I am filled with fear, yet I cannot find my way out. I have no voice. I am not sure if she is really dead or if I am really alive. I have no hope that the grave will release me. I am terrified.

When I awoke, I would remember the dream as if it were true. With slight variations, this dream came many times over a two-year period. It became part of who I was and how I dreamed. I did not try to puzzle it out or find its meaning. That would be to invite a loathsome darkness up to the conscious level, so I absorbed it, tolerated it, expected it, and hated it. It was an unwelcome part of me, just as a bad tooth is a part of me. I endured it even as I loathed it. I lived with it even as I attempted to smother it.

It was into this dark and fearsome night that a bright shower of sparks glimmered and sparkled into my subconscious. They illuminated my frightful dreams. They brightened this shadowed phantasm of dread. As sparks, they came uninvited and unannounced. They came with grace, truth, and love, revealing a baseless fear, naming a horrific lie. They came to free me from a heavy burden and to release me from my nightmare.

In this special, welcome dream (vision), a gift was given to me, and I remember this one above all the others, a gift of trust and hope and life. As I wait for the chair to be given to me, a figure appears in the distance. It is hooded and huge and menacing. I cannot make out the face. It is hidden in the folds of a dark and concealing hood. This figure, in all of its aspects, is an awful and frightful apparition. It comes toward me, reaching out for me with long and powerful arms. I shrink back, shivering and cowering in absolute panic. I can smell death on its shroud and feel its dreadful essence. I know beyond a doubt that this is death and that it has come for me. Even in my dream, I wonder if I will die in my bed that very night.

Then a wondrous thing happens. As those powerful arms press me into the blackness of itself, fear vanishes. Instead of dread, I feel love and warmth and joy being showered upon me. As I am drawn more deeply into this specter of death, I see on the other side of death a glorious sight. I see green fields and bright skies and loving people. The land beyond is brighter than the graveyard is dark. It is more joyous then the graveyard is fearful. This place is more welcoming then the grave is repulsive. I am suddenly anxious to move on to that peaceful place of welcoming happiness. Death is no more than a moment. Life continues on the other side.

Then, just as I am no longer resisting the pull of those strong arms, just as I begin to move on my own toward that land of beauty and light, just as fear and horror leave me, just as joy and love overwhelm me, just then do the arms pull me back, and a voice says to me with great love and compassion, "Not yet! You still have much to do here before you can be there. But look and see and know. You need not fear me. I am the doorway to a new and more perfect life."

When I awoke from that dream, it was as if a thousand-pound weight had been lifted off me. My experience was that of an overpowering sense of release from years of oppression. The world was brighter than I had known. A dark dream of death became a bright dream of life. What I had received while sleeping became part of me in my waking life. The peace and joy and love that I had discovered in the dream melded into me. And this joy and love did not need to be hidden in some remote and safely walled-off place within me. I no longer needed to push my fear of death to a place deep in my subconscious or deny it to myself. I was free to confront death in a new and more mature and profound way. I was free to experience a life in which joy and love and peace could have their say, in which good things might very well happen. The door that had been closed was now open, if not wide, at least a little. I could see beyond the darkness into the light. It was a shower of sparks that found me in a dream but lit up my life.

An example of this dream becoming my reality happened some years later and helped me see a shower of sparks much like the one in my dream. This shower of sparks was on the side of the road.

One Saturday, I was heading home from a summer camp where I had served as a counselor. I was to preach the following

Sunday. I guess that was the reason my mind was so open to the leading of the Spirit: I was trying to figure out where my sermon might be heading, hoping for inspiration from the Holy Spirit, fearful that nothing would come to me.

As I drove the fifty miles toward home, I reviewed the week gone by, going over the insights that had come to me as I lived with the young people from summer camp, checking my experiences for sermon possibilities.

In a flash of recognition, I knew that I had just driven past a sermon, even though I did not yet know what it was. Something had caught my eye, and I needed to find out what. I turned the car around and drove back the other way, searching for sparks, watching for any clue that would tell me what they would show me.

Then, as if by plan, there they were, sparks brightly glinting over a small house set back about fifty feet from the highway. The house was a picture-perfect home, warm and delightful and secure. It was set in the center of a large, level, green field, with flowers growing in profusion in its gardens. There were wildflowers in the meadow beyond and green hills rising up in the farther distance. It seemed ideal. But what had caught my attention, what had set this house aside as unusual, was the huge fence that was erected beside it.

The reason for the high and ugly fence seemed to be a small cemetery that was located between the house and the meadow and the green hills beyond. The graveyard had perhaps twenty gravestones showing. They looked moss-covered and old. Several mature trees lent shade to the ancient graves. It was a place of quiet rest and serene peace. Yet, to those in the house, it seemed to be an unwelcome intrusion into their lives, and they had fenced it off from their view and, thus, from themselves.

Yet, by so doing, they had shut out their view of the serene meadow, the dancing flowers, the majestic green hills, and all the beauty of the valley beyond the cemetery. Their fear of death prevented them from enjoying life. There was my sermon. It was my dream, made plain again in a shower of sparks. Sunday was saved.

REFLECTIONS ON "DREAMS OF LIFE"

The voice that spoke to me in that dream was not the voice of death. Death's voice is hidden and dark and full of fearful menace. The voice that spoke to me in that dream was a voice that spoke with authority and certain knowledge from beyond death, a voice that spoke above death, a voice that spoke from victory over death.

I believe that voice was the voice of the risen Christ, speaking to me through a dream, comforting my soul. Through him, that which had been my enemy has become a doorway I need no longer fear, a doorway through which I will one day pass to that bright new land of life.

In my youth, my experiences of death brought fear into my life. When I did not share with anyone else about my fears, those fears gained the upper hand. But Jesus knew my secret fear. At his word, they fled. I know this to be true because a shower of sparks from the bonfire of his light and life has fallen on this side of the veil, and I have seen it, experienced its power, and been freed by what it has revealed.

During my second visit to the Holy Land, I visited the Garden Tomb, site of a rock tomb where Jesus's body might have been laid after his crucifixion. As I entered that dark place of death, the impenetrable walls spoke to me of finality and hopelessness. Then, as I turned to leave, the inscription over the door, seen only as one faces the door out from the inside, read, "He is not here, he has risen."

HE IS NOT HERE

Love carries the body
    in silent grief
    through the narrow door,
    from sunlight to darkness,
    pale flesh laid on
    unforgiving stone
    as rock of
    incomprehensible
    sorrow
is rolled between
what is
    and what might have been,
the entrance sealed,
    the separation complete.
    The bereaved
    are left to contemplate
    inevitable decomposition
    of hopes believed
    and promises made.
    Yet, unheard, unseen,
    in that secret space where
    creation and destruction
    contend for the last word,
    within the eternal mystery,
    endings
    become beginnings;
    life unrestrained
    bursts forth.
    The seal no longer holds;

the rock no longer separates.

Love, in radiant surprise, emerges victorious.
Easter shines
with God's laughter.

SPARK #6

DEAD BIRD FLYING

With gentle shyness, showers of sparks can display their flashes of glory in busy city streets where, without trumpet fanfare, they can go unnoticed and unheeded. They are simply the stray embers from fires so distant they are judged to be unimportant. In the winter of 1949, such a shower fell on the street where I happened to be. The sparks descended as I was minding my own business, intent on some unimportant errand in the city. What that errand might have been I have long ago forgotten. What happened in pursuit of it I will never forget.

That particular day, a New England winter storm had filled the streets and gutters with ankle-deep, dirty slush, the unwelcome legacy of eleven inches of half-melted, unplowed snow mixed with road salt. The wind was blowing hard, switching directions in the city caverns from one moment to the next, finding flaws in each pedestrian's defenses. People hurried about their personal business hunched forward, heads sunk deep in hoods and scarves, seeking shelter from the icy blasts of frigid, arctic air.

Crossing from one side of the street to the other meant taking special care lest a passing vehicle bathe the careless pedestrian in an icy spray. It also meant taking a chance that unwary feet might be drenched if their owner stepped into an unseen hole, an unpleasant prospect on so chill a day.

This was the way it was in the city the day a tiny shower

of sparks lit up my world. While pursuing my errand, I was also fighting the wind as my course led me across Main Street. I stopped and took careful note of the street's condition, the dangers that the crossing would entail, the gutter and its depth, the traffic and its speed. I was in the process of judging how far out I would have to step to avoid engulfing my feet in slush when I saw, in the gutter, in the slush, in the cold, a little gray sparrow, on its side, motionless, apparently dead.

I do not know what strange mood I was in or what sudden impulse caused me to think twice about that particular bird. It was not as if I had never seen a dead bird before. I had worked on a poultry farm, where one of my tasks each morning was to pick up dead chickens and turkeys.

And it was not as if I stopped on my daily rounds for every animal that showed up motionless in the gutter. It was not as if I had some great compassion for injured creatures. None of that would have been true.

Yet, that day, in that winter storm, under those bitterly cold conditions, it seemed right for me to reach down into the slush, take hold of that small, wet, cold, lifeless body, lift it out of the gutter, and hold it up at eye level for my consideration.

Looking at the beauty of its form, I asked myself, *How many birds have died in this storm?* Studying the perfection of its feathers and beak and feet, I wondered again, *How many of these lovely creatures have perished in this terrible cold?* My thoughts continued: *No one will take any notice or care that this one bird has died. Yet God must take notice. Not one sparrow falls but that God notices and cares. God cares about this little bird, as unimportant as it may seem to us. God cares about life and about death, about the small as about the large, about the sick as about the well, about what seems to us to be important and about what seems to us to be unimportant.*

Holding that bird in my ungloved hand, a new thought occurred to me, so obviously unreasonable and foolish that I would have dismissed it at once had it not caught me so off-guard. Would I allow myself to think such an irrational thought? There, in the middle of the city, ready to cross its main street, in the cold and slush, with a dead bird in my hands, I decided to believe what I knew by intuition was true. God could make a dead bird come alive. God could restore this dead bird to life if God chose to do so.

So, in the grip of a bright hope, believing what I had often heard affirmed in my church, I raised the body up over my head into the wind and the cold and the snow and offered a foolish prayer on behalf of the bird. It went something like this: "Holy God, if it please you to do so, and if you are willing to do so, give this bird new life, even as you gave it life when you first created it. I know you can do this. I believe you can do this, I just don't know if you want to do this. If you say no, I will understand, but I want you to know that I believe you can do it if you choose to do it. Amen."

Into the cold city streets, along with the snow, blew a shower of sparks, carrying within them the warmth and love and care of God. The bird, which had been lying still and cold in the palms of my upraised hands, suddenly twitched, moved its head, shook its feathers, stood up on its tiny legs, tried its wings, and flew away.

I was startled. I should not have been, but the truth was that I was both startled and amazed, testimony to the fact that I did not really believe as fully as I had indicated in my prayer. Why was I surprised or amazed when the bird moved and flew? God did what I had believed God could do. It was a sign to me of my unbelief in the midst of my believing.

I was also saddened when the bird flew away. For some selfish reason, I wanted to hold on to that which I had been instrumental in healing. The bird had flown away, and with it all proof of the miracle that had just occurred. Sparks fade so quickly. Only the memory remains, and memories are open to questions and doubts and other interpretations. Like shooting stars, we can only trace where they have been, not where they are.

I was, however, joyful. God had acted in a most miraculous way. God had paid attention to my particular, individual, special, and personal prayer. God had responded to me because I had made a request. God was able to actually do what others had told me God could do. This experience proved to me what I had previously only known through the word of others. The bird flew. God smiled. My faith soared.

REFLECTIONS ON "DEAD BIRD FLYING"

I do not know if the warmth of my hands brought life back into that small, cold body, or if the bird was really and truly dead. I do not know if God used me to warm the bird or if God gave that bird new life. I do not know if God worked a life-giving miracle in that bird that day, or just in me. What I do know is that God did a wondrous thing that day. What I am sure of is that what was lifeless regained life, what could not fly flew, and what must surely parish in the gutter ascended into the sky. It also seems to me that most miracles are matters of faith anyway. In my life, it seems that God always leaves room for other answers but gives me enough evidence to sustain my faith.

I wrote the following poem long before I wrote the story. Both are true, the story more complete, the poem more focused.

AN IMPROBABLE HAPPENING

An icy winter gale
pushes me
across a slushy street.

I am not ready for the storm,
my clothing more for fall
than winter.
Thin shoes dictate
that I watch my step.
So, with eyes downcast,
I encounter
a companion to my mood,
a sparrow, seeming dead
in the gutter,
captured by the cold.
Moved by compassion,
I lift the lifeless body
in my freezing hands,
and there,
in the midst of traffic,
offer it to heaven,
begging its creator
to give it life again,
wanting to believe,
(and half believing)
that such a miracle,
if not probable,
is at least possible.
In one wonderous
moment,
The fragile bird
and my faltering faith
take wing
and fly.

SPARK #7

THE RIGHT ALTITUDE

In December of 1950, the Korean War was well under way. Some of my friends had already enlisted, while others had been drafted. Waiting for my number to be called was so unbearable that, with one of my best friends, I went to the post office recruitment office and enlisted in the air force. A year later, I was graduated from flight training and gunnery school as a tail gunner on a B-45 jet bomber. I was assigned to the 85th Bomber Squadron of the 47th Bomb Wing, at that time located in the north of England.

We were told that our mission was critical to the overall balance of power in the world. Our task was to keep the Soviet Union from attacking any part of Europe while the bulk of our ground forces were being diverted to the war in Korea. To accomplish this task, our bombers were equipped with atomic weapons. We had the capability of dropping these horrific weapons just about anywhere in Europe or western Russia. Our aircraft and the A-bombs they carried were the deterrent power the United States used to keep the Soviets at bay until our Intercontinental Ballistic Missile system could be completed and deployed.

My task as a tail gunner was relatively simple: to protect the rear of the aircraft from enemy fighters. Since, with four powerful J35 jet engines, a B-45's top speed was above 550 miles per hour, enemy fighters could only, at best, attack from the rear quarter.

Radar-enhanced twin 50-caliber machine guns were intended to provide some protection for this vulnerable spot.

The tail gunner was located in a small plastic-and-metal cabin located just above the gun turret in the rearmost portion of the aircraft. We entered our position through a hatch in the tail section, just to the rear of the bomb bay. Then we would crawl through another small hatch into the tail gunner's cabin, standing up and pulling a seat up from below and behind us to sit on. We would each make sure our parachute was hooked to the small cushion-sized package that held a life raft (should we bail out over water) and that our life vests were properly attached. We would check our communications with the crew up front and our oxygen mask and oxygen levels. When the engines were started, we would check our pressurization, say our prayers, and ride the Tornado (the B-45's nickname) backward into the wild blue yonder.

It was a lonely, frightening, sometimes boring, sometimes exciting job. Yet, for me, the one element that was always present was an unspoken dread that we might one day actually be directed to let loose upon some innocent city the massively destructive power of one of these atomic weapons. That we could, on any given flight, actually destroy a million lives in less than a second was a thought darker than I could rationally comprehend for more than a second or two.

I could, on the one hand, understand my role as tail gunner protecting our aircraft. That was a simple, honorable task in defense of our national freedoms and of freedoms everywhere. When the enemy I would be firing at was a fighter pilot firing at me, I could understand and accept that. But on the other hand, when the enemy was a million nonthreatening persons in an unfamiliar city far below me who were no more guilty than I of anything worthy of the holocaust we could unleash upon them, then my mind revolted, refusing to think further about it at all.

So, it was not until the summer of 1952, at 35,000 feet, in the tail gunner's bubble of a B-45, somewhere over France or West Germany, on a simulated atomic bomb run toward a targeted East German city in a mock response to an imagined Soviet invasion, that I entertained those forbidden thoughts and discussed my fears and trepidations with God.

I was in need of a spark, an assurance that God was with me, that I was not all alone in the tail of that aircraft. As I recall it, the spark came in the prayer/ discussion that began when I finally started paying attention to what I was actually doing. It went something like this:

Me: "I can't get my mind around this. In the bomb rack right behind me hangs a weapon with more firepower than all that was used in all of World War II. That one bomb has the power to destroy the past, present, and future of an entire city. As I look down, I see the world in all of its complexity and beauty. But I'm too high to see people. From this height, they appear smaller than ants. Perhaps that makes it easier for us to kill them like ants. That bomb is both a wonder and a horror. It is hell in a shell. What have we become if we are willing to use such a device? What's happening to us? What are we becoming? Is there any hope for us? For me? How guilty am I? For what?

God: "Your questions seem to have my name on them, even though it's been a while since we last spoke. They're good questions to ask, even if you don't get complete or satisfying answers. Thirty-five thousand feet is a splendid altitude from which to gain a perspective. Being troubled with your mission will provide you with a reality check on your motives and intentions. So, to begin with, let me ask you a simple question: why are you here?"

Me: "Do you mean in the air force or here on this aircraft on this particular mission, here and now?"

God: "No. I mean *at all*. Why are you at all?"

Me: "Oh. That certainly does cover more ground. That is a 35,000-foot question, isn't it? Mm¼well¼let's see¼you created me. More than my mother or my father, you gave me life. You ordered the world into which I was born. So, I am responsible first and finally to you for who I am and for what I do. I'm still not sure what that is. I know it must have something to do with pleasing you, with being who you want me to be. That's at the heart of the question, isn't it? Can I be here with the bomb and still be pleasing to you at the same time? Can I be doing what I am doing and consider myself humane, or faithful, or even Christian?"

God: "Can you?"

Me: "I'm not sure. Right now, I don't feel like I can. I know you must hate the way we humans treat each other, crucify one another, abuse one another, and molest one another. And this bomb, the way we threaten others with destruction and death—with hell—to protect ourselves! Can we use such an evil to promote good?"

God: "I know firsthand all about suffering, cruelty, conflict, and I do not desire to have this conflict happen, but sin continually corrupts paradise. In a fallen world, justice must confront injustice, freedom must confront oppression, and love must endure the evil that is on behalf of the good that may yet be. I personally have experienced what you only worry about, just how cruel and heartless and inhumane humans can be to one another. I have been crushed by your cruelty, hurt by your inhumanity, devastated by your destructiveness. And still I believe in you, more than you believe in yourself. I love you more than you love yourself, hope for you more than you hope for yourself, and offer to do for you more than you can ever do for yourself. Do not allow cruelty to overshadow care, nor hate, love, nor evil, goodness."

Me: "I'm not sure I can tell the difference. Is my being here part of good or evil?"

God: "Yes."

Me: "Both?"

God: "Yes. What you are doing here can be motivated by the desire to do good. That you are willing to act in so horrific a way may well keep others from acting in the same way. The threat of a terrible total retaliation may push back the dangers of actual war by either side. But that only provides time and space in which love can work to build a lasting peace."

Me: "And if we waste the time and space such a threat provides?"

God: "Then good is betrayed and evil succeeds."

Me: "It seems to me that what you are saying is this: What I am doing here becomes part of the good only if I build upon it with what is good. That is more of a challenge than an answer. What should I do? Where can I start?"

God: "What must change is not the power of nations but the hearts of humans. That is where peace finds its power. That is where the effort must be placed. Peace is more than the absence of war. It is the presence of love. And love is more powerful than your A-bomb any day. Your weapons have the power to destroy your world. My love has the power to save it."

Me: "How can I change my heart, much less the hearts or attitudes or intentions or motives of people in the world around me? I'm not very smart. I've always struggled in school. Persuasion in not my gift. You know very well that I'm no saint, no great leader, no strong speaker, and no role model. I'm really not very good at all. I'm an average sinner. You surely know that."

God: "I agree with you. I'm glad you realize how inadequate you are. That does not, however, let you off the hook. It may be a fact, but it is not an excuse. Weapons may be your business right now, but changing hearts is always my business. What you cannot do by yourself, my son can do through you. That is the only way it gets done. Being inadequate is required of those who seek peace. It keeps them dependent on me, on my son, Jesus, and on my Spirit."

Pilot: "We're beginning our descent to five thousand feet. We'll be over the English coast in about fifteen minutes. This was a good mission. Had we received the word, we would have hit the target right on schedule. Good work all around."

So my prayer, conversation, consultation with God ended, but the power of that encounter helped me to see my life from a new perspective. A shower of sparks had illuminated my future path. It still illuminates my choices.

REFLECTIONS ON "THE RIGHT ALTITUDE"

I have lived in times of war and in times of non-war, but I have never lived in a time of peace. I know the vast amounts of worldly treasure and human life we are willing to spend to win a war, just or unjust. Yet I have never known humans to spend as lavishly for the peace we fought to establish. It seems to me we never have really won a war until we have built the peace. That is the work of ordinary folk. It will never truly be achieved until the end of history. We are commissioned to carry peace with us, in us. Peace is who we are as much as what we do.

As I think back on those days and that encounter with God at 35,000 feet, I now realize that my entry into full-time Christian ministry was, in part, my response to that dialogue. It was also my attempt to justify my complicity with A-bombs by doing good. Since that conversation with God, I have had many occasions to ask God whether I am doing evil or good, to determine as best I can which side I represent at any given moment. My answer is almost always "I'm not sure," and God's answer is almost always "Yes."

The difficulties I had in separating and in choosing "good" over "evil" have allowed me to imagine the sad darkness of those solders who nailed Jesus to the cross.

IMPERIAL TAX

Hard work, long day,
storms and quakes
and lousy pay,
heavy sword,
blistering heat,
weary muscles,
tired feet,
crowd control,
digging holes
nailing bodies,
setting poles,
binding cross beams,
lifting loads,
derisive insults
from the roads,
a bit of gambling
(no great prize),
three hours to kill
while someone dies.
Such tasks as these
might well unnerve
if not performed
for those I serve.
My sworn duties,
daily borne,
uphold the oath
that I have sworn.
Their cost is high.
They take their toll:
they chill the body,
numb the soul

'til cries of suffering
and pain
come meaningless
upon my brain.
These cruelties
don't penetrate
the grim realities
of state.
Though soldiering is fine,
the fact is,
obedience levies
heavy taxes.
When duty calls,
my flesh complies.
It's always someone else who dies.

SPARK #8

GIFT FROM THE SKY

Sparks have often been unintentionally carried into my life on the lives of other people. Such sparks should be no less meaningful to me because of this practical and less-than-spectacular mode of transport, but they often are. Coming in the guise of normalcy, they can wink and glow unnoticed in my busy and self-centered routine. They can pass for no more than the sparkle of human sunlight on bits of broken glass by the roadside. It is only in my memory that some of them are able to communicate the meanings that shine within them. It is only as I reflect on some long-ago events that they light up with the truth they represent. Let me give an example of such a spark.

This one happened in England when I was serving in the United States Air Force on a base in the north of England. I was young and confident and proud to be on flying status, proud of my wings and my rank (staff sergeant), and my job as tail gunner on a jet bomber. I was especially proud of my top secret clearance and of the task our group had been given to protect Europe with our atomic weapons. Looking back, all this heady stuff combined to puff me up more than I like to admit now, and more than I was aware of at the time.

Some of my air force noncommissioned officer friends were married, and their wives had come to England to be with them. Most of these married couples lived off base in housing they rented in nearby towns. These couples made friends with local folk more often and more easily than did those of us who were living on the base. One of these couples was good enough to invite a few other NCOs from the base, myself included, to their home for regular get-togethers with local folk. I was grateful for the chance to get off base, to meet some of these people, to get some sense of how the English saw the world, the United States, and the air force, to hear war stories about the blitz and Spitfires, and to get hints about shopping in local markets.

Among the several local couples that were regulars at these social gatherings were an RAF flying sergeant and his wife. He was special in our group because he was a pilot, a cut above the rest of us. In the United States Air Force, you had to be a commissioned officer to become a pilot. In England during the Second World War and for a few years after that, NCOs flew many of the non-combat aircraft.

One of the ongoing conversations among the men at these social meetings was the comparison of the USAF with the RAF—which one was the better service and why. The flying sergeant argued that the RAF could do more with less because its members were smarter, braver, and more daring than the safety-prone and timid USAF. He used the Second World War as his proof, as well as the fact that a sergeant in the RAF could do the job of a lieutenant in the USAF.

This argument quickly dented my pride in our mission, in our aircraft, and in our flight crews. Although argued in fun, it soon took on the aspect of a very real contest, one that I was determined not to lose. Looking back on it now, I see an older and more experienced war pilot having fun with a young and relatively inexperienced tail gunner, but at the time, I saw it as the USAF against the RAF, with me as the champion of the USA. So I argued hot and heavy, no holds barred, intensely and with feeling. It was no longer fun for me; it was war.

The base where I was stationed was on the edge of the North Sea, and the weather in that area was often extremely foggy. It was so foggy, in fact, that on one occasion, they closed down a movie theater because we could not see the screen for the fog that had filtered in, testimony to the fog and the state of the theater.

On a day when the fog was again thick enough to close a movie house, I was reading in my bed in my barrack when a call came from the commanding officer of the base that I should report to him at the control tower. This was a complete surprise and a deep mystery to me. It had never occurred to me that the commanding officer even knew my name, much less would want to speak to me—I could not imagine about what. Not knowing only made the summons more threatening. I told myself I had nothing to fear, but I was fearful all the same.

When I arrived at the control tower, I was invited into a room with the commanding officer and two other officers, all of whom looked as grim as the weather. The CO asked me in somber tones, "Williams, do you know anyone in the RAF?"

Feeling like sinking into the floor, I replied in a small voice, "Yes sir, a few, sir." My mind raced over the past and my association with RAF people as I tried to discover what had happened to have that question asked of me. Nothing especially bad, illegal, or uncouth came to my mind. My RAF friends and I had had a few drinks together, had had a few heated conversations together, but nothing that would upset a CO or cause a problem.

Then I noticed a package lying on a table at one side of the room. In big, black lettering on the brown paper wrapping was sprawled my particular, singular, not-to-be-mistaken-for-anyone-else's name: "Staff Sgt. Stoddard Williams, USAF, from the RAF" it said in bold directness. My heart began to pound as I realized that the package held the answer to my question.

The CO, pointing to the package, explained that an unauthorized aircraft had entered the ultra-restricted airspace over our airfield, designated an atomic weapons secure area, had dropped down out of the fog right over the control tower, had almost hit it, had ejected a package, which fell to the ground close by the control tower, and had disappeared back into the fog before any identifying numbers could be read by the duty officer. The only thing that could be identified was an RAF signal on the aircraft. It seemed to be some older type of small British military transport. The package that had fallen from the intruding aircraft had a special name on it: mine. What could possibly be in a package delivered in so dangerous a manner on so foggy a day by so daring a pilot, to so secure an airfield, in violation of so many laws, both civilian and military?

Under the careful scrutiny of the commanding officer, I went over to the table. I am sure he was watching to see whether I seemed worried about the contents, whether I would act with guilt or apprehension, or whether I would hesitate in fear. I didn't do any of these things because I already knew who had caused the mysterious parcel to fall from heaven: the flying sergeant. I also know he was my friend.

I began to slowly remove the brown paper wrapping from the package, wondering all the while what kind of trouble I was in. When the outer wrappings were removed, an inner wrapping appeared, folded around another parcel. When unfolded, the second wrapping proved to be a huge poster that, in bright red letters, encouraged the reader to "Join the Royal Air Force." Inside the poster-wrapped parcel I found a pair of large, dirty, well-worn brogans, a hint that the USAF walked when the RAF flew. That inference was strengthened on that particular day because, while the fog had grounded our aircraft for safety reasons, an RAF pilot had made it in the worst of weather down into our highly restricted airspace and back home again. If a mere RAF sergeant could fly like that, just think what an RAF lieutenant could do.

That message was meant for me, but the commanding officer

seemed to catch some of it as well. He smiled and asked nothing more. But, because unknown persons had dropped the package from an unauthorized aircraft in a restricted air space, its contents were kept by the authorities for further examination. I never did hear anything more about it from the CO or the authorities. There was no follow-up that I know about. I choose to believe that no one wanted to give the RAF any special credit for that flight, nor did anyone want to admit that our security had been so badly breached. That package could have been a bomb. For whatever reasons, the whole incident was pushed aside by those in charge.

REFLECTIONS ON "GIFT FROM THE SKY"

It has only been lately, after retelling the story perhaps a dozen times over fifty years and missing the point each time, that my reflections have given me eyes to see. I could not believe that someone would risk his life to make a point to me, or that my personal friendship with another human being could cause that friend to put himself at risk to show me his point of view. In all my pride and self-centered puffing, I did not believe with my life as he believed with his life. His wit and bravery called me out, confronted me by name, asked more of me, and laughed with me about it afterward.

There is a spark in this story, hidden for years, that has finally revealed itself to me. This story is not a once-in-a-lifetime happening. It happens every day. I have a friend, Jesus, who knows my name, who risks himself for me, and who calls me by my name, enters into the dangerous, restricted areas of my life, crosses the borders of safety, dares the thick fog of ignorance and sin, finds me where I am, to my surprise, and gives me gifts from heaven, God's packages of mercy and grace. My name is on these packages, written in bold letters. I can open these treasures of faith and love without guilt or fear or apprehension because they come from a friend. They fall daily near my control tower, waiting for me to open them, to see once again that his friendship counts, that he is more friend to me than I am to him, that he risks more for me than I do for him, and that when the fog clears and the sun comes out, we will sit and talk and laugh about it together. That's what friends do.

The past may still to be mined for treasures of truth that will add value to our present and thus help shape our futures. Past sparks can and do light present fires.

There was a sense of love and caring in that gift package from the sky. It was delivered through real danger, with great daring, to an average guy like me. Such a gift built me up and yet caused me to feel my smallness, all at the same time. That is how I stand before God: amazed at who I am and, at the same time, aware of who I am not. The package was more about the one who sent it than about the one who had received it.

After I retired from the settled ministry, my wife and I moved to Cape Cod. Almost every day, we would spend time at our favorite beach. Part of that beach time was spent finding small, smooth stones that were worn down to gemlike beauty by sand, tide, and wind. God has allowed life's hard places to work the rough edges off me. That process is far from over. Thus, this poem.

BROKEN

Here upon the beach I stand,
Sea-smoothed pebbles in my hand,
glacier-gouged from granite land,
not still boulder,
not yet sand.
Sea winds sculpt

and storm waves guide
the sands
that on their currents ride.
Just so, my stony parts
must be
broken by
what tempers me,
God's word my wind,
God's will my sea.

But, like these pebbles, here I stand,
Still somewhat small,
still somehow grand,
willful heart with willing hand,
not still boulder, not yet sand.

SPARK #9

JOINED IN SPIRIT

As a full-time, settled pastor, my first parish was in a small, rural, conservative Connecticut town that disconnected itself from the rest of the world along the banks of the Connecticut River. At the time I was graduating from seminary, the Congregational church of that town called me to serve as their full-time pastor. I received the call gladly, for that church was a historic institution with a beautiful building, though its influence rested more on an illustrious past than on its unremarkable present. In spite of that, the congregation proved to be supportive, encouraging, and helpful to me, their new and untried pastor. I was proud to receive their call and have my ordination ceremony held in their lovely church.

The parsonage that they provided with the call was a spacious old home built around 1830. It had wide floorboards, old plumbing, a marvelous stairway, and a walk-in fireplace in the kitchen. It was beautiful, charming, and suited our furniture very well. Much of that furniture was the hand-me-down variety that looked antiquated.

I loved the house and its authentic, historic charm. It seemed to impute importance to my position as pastor. It was my wife, however, who had to keep it clean and neat. With a dirt cellar, and windows that put up no defense against outside grime, keeping our home dusted and polished proved to be a huge job. On top of that, the trustees paid regular visits to see how their property was prospering under my stewardship and my wife's diligent housekeeping.

Relying on the strength of my ignorance and pomposity, I was able to ignore the fact that this was, after all, my wife's first experience as the wife of a settled minister—a duty she fulfilled very well, but not without some tension.

Adding to the weight on her shoulders, while I was still in seminary, we had taken an eight-year-old boy into our home to live with us for a while. This boy's father, my mother's brother, had suffered a massive coronary artery failure and had died a traumatic and early death. His wife, never fully at ease in this world, was admitted to an institution to be treated for a mental breakdown. That left three boys without parents. My wife and I elected to help out for a while by taking the youngest boy to live with us.

This meant that my wife had not only the newly acquired role of minister's wife and the task of caretaker of the church manse, but she also had the hard task of caring for an eight-year-old boy who had plenty of problems of his own.

As for me, I took it for granted that my wife would participate at the church, act as mistress of the manse, mother an eight-year-old who had emotional trauma, and be a proper caretaker of historic and valuable church property. Not only did I invite her to do all this, but I expected her to do it with good humor, engineering efficiency, and boundless energy while I tended to the "important" matters of pastoring the church.

In addition, someone had given us a big red setter dog. It had developed a bad front leg and was no longer suited to show. Shortly after we took control of "Lady Jane," she became romantically involved with a black Lab and presented us with thirteen puppies. I was sure that my wife could add this to her list of responsibilities without being overburdened.

So it was that tensions built up slowly between my wife and myself. Nothing horrific, mind you, just small stuff that made our relationship uncomfortable for both of us. Looking back on it with the advantage of hindsight, I am sure that the fault for these tensions lay in my uncaring attitude, in my unsympathetic assumption that my wife would do anything I expected of her, complete any task the church set for her, live up to the expectations that our families had erected for her, and do so without my enthusiastic and encouraging support.

We had lived in this atmosphere of tension and disagreement for three or four months when the pressure grew so great that it exceeded the limits of our civility and the gasket of our togetherness blew. The precipitating argument was over some small thing that, under ordinary circumstances, would not have caused more than a gentle ripple. I cannot recall what it was about, even though it did seem to be world-shaking at the time.

The outcome of our strongly worded exchange of vastly differing views, pressurized by volatile emotions, led to a shouting match of hurt feelings and angry accusations. In frustration and self-pity at being so misunderstood in my rightness, I went to sulk in the front parlor. My wife, with whatever violent or violated feelings she may have had, rushed up the stairs to our bedroom and loudly slammed the door, her last word of our conversation.

Now I was alone, isolated, and miserable. In my self-inflicted isolation, I was free to muck about in my self-centered concern, weighing my rightness against her wrongness, tasting the bitterness expressed and the love neglected.

But soon, as the moments quieted into reflection and my feelings cooled down toward reason, none of that "right or wrong" stuff seemed to matter nearly as much as the fact that my wife was upstairs, angry and hurt, and I was, somehow, the source of her distress. My spirit was also in pain because my pride would not acknowledge my wrongness.

Still, because of the situation, or maybe in spite of it, I was led to pick up my Bible. An inner voice, ever so remote and hard to hear through the roaring tumult of my feelings, seemed to invite me to turn to First Kings, the fourth chapter, the twenty-fourth verse.

In reluctant obedience to this vague leading, and hoping for a word of wisdom from the Word of God, a word that would prove me right, I turned to the scripture that was indicated. As I often do when following that small, inner voice, I felt a bit silly and superstitious for Bible dipping, but I followed the urge anyway. And the verse read: "For he had dominion over all the region west of the Euphrates from Tephsah to Gaza, over all the kings west of the Euphrates; and he had peace on all sides."

My response to that scripture was just what most other people's would have been: *What has this got to do with anything?* My hope of a saving or encouraging word faded to zero. I was convinced that I was just inventing religious things to do by hiding behind scripture and finding help where none was to be found.

But, win or lose, right or wrong, faithful or unfaithful, I determined that I would share this failed scriptural search with my wife, if for no other reason than to indicate I was at least trying to be helpful and doing what pastors were supposed to do—search the scriptures.

So, up the stairs I went, listening for the kind of sounds that might warn me about the condition my wife was in—sad, remote, and willing to talk. I knocked on the door lightly, filled with trepidation and fear that my knock would be unwelcome, that my presence on the second floor would be hotly rejected.

To my surprise, her voice sounded welcoming and calm as she invited me to enter. "Come on in. I have something to share with you," she said in a voice totally lacking in anger or hurt. I went in and sat down on the bed beside her. She had stolen my thunder. She had her Bible in her hand.

I tried to get my message in first. "I was led to look at scripture," I began, but she cut me off before I could finish.

"So was I," she said, "but I can't make much out of it. It seemed to me that I was to look at First Kings, four, twenty-four, but it makes no sense to me at all. You're the Bible expert. Perhaps you can figure it out."

Before she could show me the place in her Bible where she had found the scripture, I held out my Bible with my finger in the same exact book, the same exact chapter, the same exact verse. "I have just now read that same exact scripture. I was led to it, just as you were."

We sat in stunned silence. The real enormity of that event did not sink in for several long moments. What were the odds that two separated people with different needs, on different floors, with different perspectives, out of different backgrounds, with different training, neither of whom knew what the other was going to do, would pick out the same book, the same chapter, and the same unfamiliar and seemingly irrelevant verse?

The odds of that happening would be astronomical, beyond coincidence or chance. Surely this was a spiritual sign, a word, and a gift to us from God. Even while we were being separated by so many other things, we were together in the Word and in the Spirit and in the mind of God. But what did God intend for us to understand by joining us back together in so unlikely and mystical a manner? It would take years for the meaning of that amazing spiritual event to even begin to clarify for me. At the very least, God was saying that our togetherness was to be founded on our love of God and of God's Word, and that our common unity and understanding depended upon our being together in the Word. To me, God was saying that my ministry depended on both my wife and me, not just on me, and that I was to care for her as I cared for myself. That I could not take her for granted or expect her to do things because of my unexpressed expectations or the expectations of others. That our choosing and our doing were to be motivated by our love of God and in obedience to God's Word. And finally, that one of us alone would not be able to understand or do as much as the two of us together could accomplish when we were together in our spirits.

REFLECTIONS ON "JOINED IN SPIRIT"

I still behold with awe and wonder that very special afternoon when, sitting next to my wife on the bed, she and I were drawn past our disagreements by the mystical work of the Holy Spirit. I am amazed that God gave to each of us the same specific and singular scripture, scripture that neither of us individually could understand. I am astounded and grateful that when we come together in our common seeking, we could quickly and easily understand the meaning of it. When I remember those special and precious gifts (sparks), I am reminded once again that my wife and I are together under the mercy and grace of a loving God who does not want us to be separated by my self-centered carelessness or self-righteous isolation. I have God's word on that: the God of all places and all people desires *peace on all sides.*

As I discovered that God is more constant and trustworthy than any of my opinions or feelings or desires, that was the beginning of wisdom for me. That God could speak through my wife, even when she was "wrong" and I was "right"—that was the beginning of matrimonial humility for me. So much of what we learn depends on where we are going and to whom we are listening. How we read our compass tells us where we are and where we are headed.

THE COMPASS

When our hand
is on the tiller
and our sails
are hoisted high
and the compass
that we follow
shows the north
we travel by,
it would help
if we'd remember
that the ship
on which we sail
may distort
the needles pointing,
and its accuracy may fail,
for the iron
in our shipmates
and the steel
within ourselves
may add
further deviations
to the twisting
of the swells.
We may check
with other vessels,
other sailors, other charts,
for we're told more
by the total
than we are
by just the parts.
We must trust

the hope that's in us
that's beyond
our compass small
we can somehow
trust the promise
that is part of every call
of a power that flows
more constant
than a magnet's
back and forth,
a power that is within us,
a love that is true north.

SPARK #10

THE PENNY

Sparks can sometimes cast new light on the beauty and splendor of ordinary, everyday things—things that would not normally be noticed or appreciated by people like me. Sparks can draw our attention to what we might otherwise miss. Like the singular importance of a penny in God's provision. This story is about such a spark, such a penny.

During the 1980s in the church where I was then serving as pastor, a small but significant group of men had formed a men's fellowship. The times were full of dynamic challenges, conflicts, and confrontations. Along with their growing sensitivity to the many social issues that were bubbling all about us, these men were asking hard questions about their use of talents and resources in our church. This group was also involved in the movement of the Holy Spirit in our congregation through the reawakening of Evangelical fervor and Pentecostal renewal, which had begun for us in the 70s. It was in this social and theological ferment that those in the group found themselves struggling with such questions as "How do we serve God here and now?" and "How do we worship God, here and now?" and "What can we truly believe about God here and now?" It was into this little corner of God's searching church that a spark descended.

Twice a year in the normal course of events, this men's group would put on a supper for church members, friends, and neighborhood folk. It was a splendid affair and was eagerly looked forward to by many. The men would get together about two months before the supper was be held to plan out the menu and decide who would do publicity, who would buy what, who would get the tickets out—all the things that past experience and common sense indicated we needed to do.

It was at one of these planning meetings that, in the midst of our small talk and friendly chatter, a particularly gritty question surfaced. It was, "Are we trusting in God's help as we plan this supper? Are we asking God all the questions we should ask, questions concerning what food to serve and what day to have it and whom God would have us invite to be our speaker?" As a pastor, I felt that I should have a significant theological reflection to put forward, uplifting answers to offer, but I did not have a clue. And the question got more basic still. "Is God really a part of this dinner effort, or is God just a benevolent onlooker?" The men did not seem to want a philosophical or theological statement; they were not looking for God-led answers.

As the question shaped itself in us and for us, I could feel a flush of guilt and embarrassment rush through me. I sensed that within their spirits, these men were seeking for new and stronger ways to trust God. I was all too aware that I turned to God only when my own resources ran out. I was conscious of the troubling reality that if there were no unsolvable problems in my life, I felt no need to trust God with my everyday activities. I, myself, was not turning to God when things went smoothly, only when things went badly. This whole discussion was underlining my own weakness.

For these men, now that the question had been raised and explored, simply trusting God in a general and non-specific way was no longer adequate. Much to my dismay, they were being pushed by the question to go further. They had a sense that more was being required of them. And if this trust was required of them, how much more of me, their pastor? As the group considered these things, we were led to seek out a new and more specific way of trusting God in the planning of the meal.

As we talked, we discovered that we were reluctant to name a specific for fear that God would not follow through. Better to keep it general so that God could not disappoint us. For instance, if we asked God to make sure that the dinner would have 200 people attending, that would be measurable. If only 190 showed up, we would feel that our prayer was only partially answered. Our faith would be tested, and we would end up trusting God less or believing that our faith was just too weak to produce the desired answer.

As for me, I was willing to ask God for a parking place at the mall once in a while, but always silently and never in the presence of another person. I would never put God or my faith to a public test. In my mind, it would be presumptive of me to think that God would devote time to my little and unimportant needs. I would pray for people to be healed or comforted or helped, but I would always add, "if it be your will." Thus, in my insecurity, using this phrase, I let God and my faith off the hook.

Well, to my dismay and silent disapproval, the men decided to ask God for a very specific item as a test of their faithfulness. They decided to put themselves and God out on a limb. This is how they decided to do it. At the supper, baskets would be placed on all the tables. Into these baskets guests would be asked to place their contributions toward the expenses of the meal. The group decided that anything over the amount of our expense would be set aside to help pay for some Bibles we had decided to give away at our church booth at the town fair. We had checked to find out what the American Bible Society charged for the Bibles we needed. We decided to order three boxes.

With this in mind, the group decided to ask God to move those present to give enough in the free will offering so that the cost of the meal and speaker would be covered and the Bibles would be paid for. There would be no need to spend any money from our general fund. Several of the men emphasized that we were asking God for all the money to cover the cost of the Bibles, not part of it.

Although I was dubious about their plan, or the chances of our collecting that much money, I was impressed by their sincerity and courage. I felt like a bandleader standing on the sidelines, watching while the band tries a new piece of music. I felt like saying, "Wait for me! I'm your leader."

So the day finally came when we were to put on the supper. The group gathered at the church, prepared the food, and set up the tables. Our treasurer kept a careful record of everything that was spent on the food and decorations. To those well-documented expenses we then added the known cost of the three boxes of Bibles. With this figure in mind, we stood around the kitchen table, and I prayed something like this: "Please, God, we pray that you will bless the work of our hands and the intentions of our hearts in this event. Bless those who attend and the message given. Bless the food and the fellowship. May Jesus receive all the glory and honor in what we do here. And, Holy God, bless the hearts of those present that their donations may not only cover the cost of this dinner but also the cost of the three boxes of Bibles that we intend to give away at our town fair. We thank you in advance for granting us this gift. Amen." I was going to add "if it be your will," but thought better of it.

Having thus committed our faith to prayer, we went about serving the meal and enjoying the speaker's presentation. But I did so with a certain uneasiness and with an eye on the baskets. I already had misgivings about my participation in the process and about my offering of that particular prayer. Ordinarily, I prayed for such things as healing and support and distant conflicts and unmeasurable miracles, but never for a need so articulated and specific that God could be held accountable for the answer. This was new ground, and I was an uneasy pilgrim.

I had somehow encouraged these men to believe God for a

specific dollars-and-cents amount. How would God respond to so brazen a challenge? Were we trusting God, or were we testing God? What would I say when the amount raised was, as it must be, over or under the amount requested in the prayer? What would the men say about me for leading them in such a questionable direction?

So the speaker concluded, and the request was made that those present make a free will contribution toward the expenses of the evening and that they place them in the baskets provided. As they did so, I watched the baskets fill with dollars as my mind filled with dark thoughts. There were not enough people there to give the kind of money we needed, I thought. The food was not fancy enough to get them to make large enough contributions. Our expenses were so large that there would be little left over. So my negative thoughts prepared me for the worst.

The people left. The dishes were brought to the kitchen, and we washed and dried them. The hour was late when finally we gathered around the baskets to count the money. The total was finally announced. We had collected $432.53. Expenses were totaled at $164.27. That left us with $268.26 for the Bibles. The treasurer reminded us that the cost of the Bibles was only $251.16. Although God had met our need with some $17.10 to spare, still the amount had not been exact. That gave us no reason to doubt God. Had not God been more than generous, exceeding my fearful expectations by a mile? But the prayer request still hung in the air, on the edge of being affirmed, on the edge of being denied.

Then a remarkable thing happened, so remarkable that it shook me to my spiritual roots. The treasurer, not wanting to find God in the wrong, had reexamined his paperwork to see if the discrepancy might actually be his and not God's. This, I thought, was possible, but unlikely. As the group worked to make sense of the results of the amount of the collection, the treasurer spoke up in a voice filed with awe. He said, "Guys, I forget to add in shipping and handling. The shipping and handling for three boxes of Bibles will be $17.10. So, we do have the amount of money we need to pay for the Bibles, exactly, to the penny."

God had known our needs more specifically than we did. Our prayer has been answered, to the penny.

REFLECTIONS ON "THE PENNY"

I do not believe God needs to answer my prayers to the penny every time. Not even very often. The problem is not with God's response but with our prayers. But to know that God can and does know and care about the dollars and the pennies of our lives is a reality that just overwhelms me. In that small event on that rather trivial occasion, God was leading us into a deeper faith at the very heart of our believing.

I needed to know in a more profound way that God was available to me specifically, particularly, individually, and not just for the larger (dollar) issues of life, but also, and more importantly, for the smaller (penny) ones as well. God does know the hairs on my head as well as the needs of war-torn countries. And because this is so, because God proves faithful in my penny issues of life, I can more confidently pray to God about the dollar issues of my life and the life of the world. I may not turn to God in every little circumstance for every little thing, but God does care about every little thing and will bend to meet my specific needs exactly. I began to learn this in that men's group back in my early days of pastoring and have been learning it more fully ever since.

When I will not pay attention to God, God comes to me. When humankind will not pay attention to God, God comes to humanity. God descends in so many ways that I am sure I miss most of them. I am just like my grandchildren. They do not listen to me when they are involved in a game of pool in the basement and I speak to them from the top of the stairs. Sometimes, I just have to go down to where they are.

DESCENDING

Grandchildren
in the basement,
queue sticks in hand,
hard at play,
escaping heat, boredom,
and adults,
intent on their game.
From upstairs I call down to
them,
my voice easily heard
above the click of balls
and the little arguments
competition produces.
No response.
Their game continues.
Hearing,
they have chosen not to
listen.
Annoyed and hurt,
I endure their indifference.
I am tempted to shout,
but that would only
make me angrier
and them more distant still.
I will descend to them,
speak softly,
interpose myself

between them
and their game,
hoping that,
seeing the voice that calls,
they will respond to me
and not to some
disembodied order
from upstairs.
Love may draw them
close enough
to hear.
It is worth the trip.

SPARK #11

FISHING EXPEDITION

After twenty years as pastor of a church in Connecticut, I was granted a second sabbatical by that church for recreation and education. Because our family had experienced a full measure of love, acceptance, and personal growth on our first sabbatical in Hawaii, we decided to return there for a second time. The church where I had spent most of my first sabbatical as interim pastor was located on the island of Kauai, in the town of Kappa. As God would have it, that very same church needed another interim at the time of my second sabbatical. I contacted them, and they seemed most willing, even excited, to have me back again. We were equally excited to be invited to return.

The membership of that church was predominantly Japanese. The way they chose to express their Christianity was strongly influenced by their culture. Beyond culture, the stamp of the missionary movement that had shaped their faith in years long past was still very evident. In addition, these members were working out their Christian faith in a town that had over thirty major religious communities among its varied and multicultural population. Because of the context in which they lived their daily lives, their theology was sometimes uniquely mixed with overtones of other philosophies and theologies. In the midst of all this, however, their outreach was strong, their prayer life faithful, and their fellowship vibrant and church-centered. It was an exciting place to serve.

Into this community of somewhat non-mainstream but committed and faithful Japanese Christian brothers and sisters my family and I entered for a second time. My mission, as defined by their leadership (and by St. Paul), was to preach Jesus and him crucified. The worship was simple, evangelical, and well attended. The message was eagerly received, and the congregational response was gratifying.

Along with preaching, leading worship, teaching, and attending meetings, there was considerable time for our family to explore the island, enjoying the beautiful scenery and learning about the varied cultures and histories of the local people, and so we did.

One of the things I had wanted to do on my first trip to the Islands was to go deep-sea fishing. I had gone reef walking but had never gone out on a boat for the big fish. So, on this second trip, I asked the deaconate if they knew of an inexpensive way for me to fish for the big fish.

It was, therefore, no surprise to me when one of the deeply committed deacons asked me if I would be willing to tell her husband about Jesus in exchange for a fishing trip. She could, she said, get her husband to invite me on one of his fishing trips. He owned a thirty-five-foot deep-sea fishing boat. Her hope was that I would I go out with him and, while fishing, bring up the story of Jesus. She told me that her husband was a nominal Buddhist who was not at all interested in his wife's religion or her stories about her faith. She thought that just perhaps he would listen if a man spoke to him about such things. She had tried with no success. At least, she said, I would get a fishing trip out of it if I was willing. I was.

She was true to her word; two weeks later, I received an invitation from her husband to go fishing with his helper and with him. It seemed to be a less-than-wholehearted invitation, but an invitation nonetheless. I met them at the pier with visions of a full day of deep-sea fishing in my mind.

It was an older boat, somewhat in need of paint, but, all things considered, a good-looking and well equipped vessel. I climbed aboard, shook hands with the husband (captain) and his friend (mate), and we were off.

From the very beginning, it was obvious that I was not really a welcome guest. My passage had obviously been gained by the wife's insistence, not by the husband's enthusiasm. It seemed that I was just in the way, sand in a well-greased routine. They went about the business of running the boat and preparing the fishing gear by speaking only Japanese, looking only at one another, and giving no notice to my presence in the rear of the boat. I knew the captain spoke rather good English. I did not believe the mate spoke much English at all.

I sat and watched them at their tasks, listened to their chatter, and thought how difficult it was going to be to tell them anything at all, much less anything about Jesus. It's always hard to be an unwanted guest. It's harder still to be so among people whom you do not know, who speak a different language, celebrate a different religion, come from a different culture, and are far more likely to see you as an intruder than as a guest.

Yet, if I was their problem, that was my problem. I was, in fact, intruding on their space, on their day, on their outing. I was a Christian pastor with a strong desire to fish and with a secret Christian agenda to speak about Jesus. What could I do there? I wondered. Why had God arranged for me to be there, opened the door, smoothed the way? Being a missionary was far more difficult than I had imagined. But the deal was of my making, and the opportunity was at hand.

It was then, just as the weight of my promise to speak about Jesus was dragging me down, that a well-worn saying came to my mind: "When all else fails, pray." So I prayed as I sat and watched the two strangers at their labors. I prayed, in spite of the negative thoughts darting through my mind. I prayed, in spite of the impossible task that pointed me beyond my capabilities. I prayed a soul-deep prayer of faith, nurtured by the seeming impossibility of my situation. I prayed, "Dear Jesus, I do not know how to witness to this man. I'm not sure I even want to. But I have given my word, and I trust you to provide the way. I am ready to do whatever you lead me to do, even if it means my very life. If you need to, sink this boat that your glory may be shown." At that moment, I meant that prayer as completely as any prayer I had ever prayed, totally and without reservation.

That bold prayer was no sooner prayed, the last syllable offered to God, not a millisecond having passed, than the sea directly behind the boat exploded with a loud crashing sound and the whole boat began to shudder and tremble and vibrate as if it had been struck by a torpedo. The captain rushed to the controls and pulled back the throttle. The engine speed decreased, the prop slowed, and the trembling and shaking of the boat eased.

No sooner had we lost speed than we also lost rudder control, the boat turning sideways to the huge, twenty-foot, mid-ocean waves. We were carried along with the current northward toward Alaska, some two thousand miles away. As soon as the captain tried to increase the engine speed, the boat would shake and shudder in a manner that would, if continued, cause it to come apart in no time at all. So, the choice was whether to slow down and be either scuttled by the waves or pushed past the tiny island of Kauai into the vast ocean beyond, or to increase speed, head for Kauai, and be shaken to pieces on the way.

When I looked up, the captain and his mate were wearing life jackets, drawn forth from some secret place under the front deck. I motioned to him that I would like to have one also, and he tossed one to me as well. Had that been a test of my trust that God would save us? I wondered.

It was clear to me that neither captain nor crew had any idea what to do. Nor did I. So I decided to do what I could do. It was too late for stories about Jesus. I shouted to them, "I will pray to Jesus." That was all I could do—pray. I was not even sure they had heard me, much less paid any attention to me. It seemed such a limp and empty offer to make at such a crucial time. But it was better than nothing.

So I prayed, "O Lord, help this man figure out what to do next." And as I prayed, the captain seem to get a new thought.

"I'll rig a sea anchor," he said to the two of us with the conviction of a newfound hope. "That will allow me to steer the boat at the very slow speed at which I can safely spin the prop."

A sea anchor is a bucket tied to a rope and dragged behind the boat to help steer it. If the boat wants to turn left, the bucket is dragged on the right side to help turn the boat effectively. Without the use of a sea anchor, the boat would only go in a large circle. With the sea anchor, we could manage to go in a somewhat straight line toward shore. He fixed a sea anchor to the rear of the boat, and we began to move toward shore.

But time was also a factor. If we did not make shore before the current carried us beyond the island, we would be swept into the ocean north of Kauai. This was bad, the captain warned us. Once we were carried that far north, no one would know where to look for us.

"Why not just radio the coast guard and tell them we need help?" I asked him.

"Because the radio is in the repair shop," was his troubling reply.

His next admission told me even more about the seriousness of our condition. "I'm very worried," the captain said with some feeling, "because I have no insurance on my boat right now." It was clear to me that he felt his boat was in danger of being lost. The loss of passengers did not seem to concern him as much as the loss of his boat. We would not sink. Our life jackets would help us float until we were rescued. His boat could sink.

My recent prayer came rushing back to me in stark relief. I had prayed, and meant it, that if God wanted to sink the boat, he should do so. Did God now intend to do just that? It was a prayer I was no longer sure I meant now that we were in real and deadly danger. But, if prayer had been my option then, it was still my option now.

So, again I said to the captain, "I'll pray." And I did, with energy and feeling: "Jesus, get us to the shore before we are lost to the sea or sunk by the waves." And, slowly but surely, with the help of the sea anchor, we were able to inch our way toward the shore, even as we were being carried northward toward Alaska by the strong ocean current and the huge ocean waves.

Now, the north end of the island of Kauai is a region of steep cliffs and sharp rocks. There is no place there for a boat to safely land. There are, however, many dangerous places where the relentlessly crashing surf can easily dash a boat to pieces upon sharp lava rocks. It was toward these steep cliffs and sharp rocks that we were slowly making our way. If we did not make the inhospitable rocks, no other shore was available, only the wide sea beyond.

As we drew near that threatening cliffs, the pounding of the surf upon those terrible rocks sent fear trembling through my heart. "We must let down our anchor before we're crushed upon the rocks," the captain said, "but the water will be too deep for the anchor to catch the bottom until we get in very close to the rocks. It will be very dangerous. We will need to be very lucky." Was it better to drown in the open ocean or to be dashed to pieces on rocks? I wondered.

As we approached the treacherous rocks and the pounding surf, the captain could wait no longer, and he dropped the anchor. To no avail. The anchor did hit bottom, but it did not hold. Each wave rushing beneath the boat lifted us up and pushed us on, ever nearer the rocks. Captain and mate were helpless to do anything but await the inevitable disaster. I could do one thing more—I could pray, and so I did. "Jesus, we made it this far with your help.

Save us now from the surf and the rocks. Let the anchor hold." This time, I prayed aloud so that, should they be paying attention to me, they might hear and give God the glory.

Immediately upon my offering that prayer, the anchor line suddenly became taut, the anchor took hold, the boat swinging bow-first toward the shore, secure, stationary, safe from the rocks. Where we had come to rest was no more than ten feet from the rocky edge of destruction.

Still, how were we to get ashore or save the boat or notify our families or get help? There were, the captain assured me, no people who lived in this inaccessible and deserted part of the island. But, unmoved by that fact, I prayed that someone would notice us. Beginning to believe in the power of my prayers, I stood up on the front deck and waved my life preserver for anyone to see, if they were there. We could see no one at all. Then I prayed aloud again: "Lord, send us someone to see us and notify the authorities." No sooner had the prayer left my lips than a person appeared on the porch of a small house on the shore, hidden and all but invisible from where we were, and waved back at us.

That done, we waited, eating a very late lunch that had been packed for us by the thoughtful wife. In about forty-five minutes, a coast guard cutter appeared to throw us a line, tug us away from the shore, and pull us to a landing on the far side of the island. I was late for supper and had no fish. But I did have a story about Jesus.

REFLECTIONS ON "FISHING EXPEDITION"

When I went to Hawaii, I did so, in part, to help our denomination train church members in a program called "Do and Tell Evangelism." I went, therefore, with the expectation that I would be teaching and telling, not learning and listening. I had accepted that trip out to sea as an unwelcome passenger on an uninsured boat with two non-Christians with the secret agenda of telling them about Jesus. That was my intention. God, on the other hand, used the trip to teach me about the reality of my own faith, to teach me to believe what I said, and to teach me to trust the Jesus for whom I would be a witness. God isolated me in a place where no other communications were possible, where the only language available to me was the language of prayer.

I do not have a very sharp learning curve, and I am often extremely unreceptive concerning those things God is trying to teach me. It was for my sake more than for theirs that God arranged for me go spend time with those dear men. I am not sure how well I witnessed to them on that unhappy voyage. What I do know is that God witnessed to me in a most profound way. What I remember most vividly is that millisecond between my prayer and the explosion at the rear of the boat. It was as if God had said to me, "Take care about that for which you pray. Mean it, because I may answer your prayer, and quicker than you may think." God caught me when I thought I was the one who was going fishing.

God is a Fisher God, seeking with bait and hook to save us from ourselves for the kingdom. So, this poem.

FISHER GOD

My fisher God, with bait and rod,
with hook and line, has sought me.
With my own sin, God reeled me in;
then, with Love's net, God caught me.

It seems absurd, yet at God's word
I fish so God can get them.
Forgiven sin will reel them in,
and Love will finally net them.

SPARK #12
ROOT AND BRANCH

It was during this same sabbatical in Hawaii that a spark lit up a certain passage of scripture in a new light, giving a depth of meaning that was not there for me before. This new measure of understanding concerned one of Jesus's agrarian illustrations, the one about him being the vine and his followers being the branches. In the Gospel of John, the fifteenth chapter, Jesus says,

> Abide in me as I abide in you. Just as the branch cannot bear fruit by itself unless it abides in the vine, neither can you unless you abide in me. I am the vine, you are the branches. Those who abide in me and I in them bear much fruit, because apart from me you can do nothing.

My understanding of this scripture came alive for me on the island of Kauai when sparks of God's story fell upon my story.

The early beginnings of a "Pacific islands garden" were being planted by a member of the church where I was serving as a supply pastor. This far-sighted and hardworking Japanese American had a beautiful vision of a garden that would showcase all the plants and trees that grew on Pacific islands. Such a garden would take a long time to develop, but he was in the process of taking the first steps in that direction.

At his wife's invitation, my wife and I made an afternoon visit to this future garden paradise. There were, we saw, many kinds of plants scattered about in various-sized and shaped pots. In addition, there were all kinds of shrubs and trees in various stages of growth newly planted around his five-acre plot. In front of his open-air greenhouse, practically covering the ground, we could see about a hundred or more small containers. What made these especially interesting to me was the fact that each pot was filled with soil that had, sticking up out of it, the stubby, cut-off stem of some unknown plant. Nothing alive or green showed, only the bare, five-inch stem protruding from the dark, volcanic soil.

Why did my host have all those cut-off plants? I asked myself. My confusion must have been showing because the gardener said to me, "This is a strange way to plant a garden, is it not? Would you like an explanation?" I replied that I was curious and would appreciate knowing more about those strange pots with their solitary stems. He explained to us that Kauai soil was mostly volcanic. This unusual soil was inhospitable to other plants from other islands, and they just could not grow or prosper in it. To make it possible for him to grow plants foreign to this island on this island, he was going to graft them onto the stems of plants that could and did prosper in this special soil. The root systems of these stems would nourish the grafted plants and enable them to succeed in this strange place. Root would give nourishment and life to plant, and plant would give blossom and fruit to root, and the two would become one by living together in biotic sharing.

There and then, in the midst of that future garden, in the facts of the explanation given, among those exceptional pots and stems, a spark of God's divine love descended.

The third chapter of Ephesians sprang to my mind as if spoken by the Spirit:

I pray that, according to the riches of his glory, he may grant that you may be strengthened in your inner being with power through his Spirit, and that Christ may dwell in your hearts through faith, as you are being rooted and grounded in love.

Here I was, looking at a real-life example of exactly that to which St. Paul was referring. Jesus is the vine (stem), and we are the plants (branches). It is through Jesus that we find the root system that nourishes us in love. With Jesus, we can now grow in soil in which we could not otherwise prosper (strangers in a strange land, in the world but not of it). Without the roots supplied to us in Jesus, we could not bear much fruit or find the fullness of life. With Jesus, we are rooted and grounded in the strange and foreign soil of love.

REFLECTIONS ON "ROOT AND BRANCH"

This spark came to me while the gardener was explaining to me the wonderful way he was planting his garden. Even while he was centered on his garden, God centered me on God's garden. One story suddenly linked to another, one garden linked to another, one gardener linked to another. So do holy sparks fly from the great fire of God's love across the centuries to light little fires in our time, in our lives, in our understanding, uniting the present with the past, the contemporary word with the eternal Word.

Such sparks continue to teach me that because God is real, God is constantly to be rediscovered in the reality of everyday life, everyday things, everyday events. God is not so supernatural that God cannot be touched in the very nature of the world in which we live. Holy sparks fly, holy fires burn, truth recites God's story, and we who sit around the bonfire listen with hope and joyfully watch the sparks fly.

In new words for the hymn "He Leadeth Me," I have tried to blend the natural with the supernatural, every time-controlled day with timeless eternity. These dimensions were often highlighted as we sought our way to completing a special home we could call our own. As we had the time and the money, we worked on our little Wick's precut cabin in the woods. It was a slow but satisfying effort. Slow because everything I did needed to be done twice—once wrong and the second time right. Satisfying because it was a retreat where we could go with our children for **Wind, Water, Earth, and Fire.**

WIND, WATER, EARTH, AND FIRE

As wind,
now let your Spirit breathe
new truth into what we believe.
Our faltering
trust and hope revive
with Breath
that keeps our faith alive.

[Refrain:]
Come, Spirit,
all our hearts inspire
through wind and water,
earth and fire,
the splendor of
God's grace proclaim
by glories shown
in nature's frame.

As water,
let God's Spirit fall,
that holy rain may bless us all.
Cleanse every sin,
wash every face,
refresh us
with redeeming grace.

As earth,
in which your people toil
to plant and grow
in your rich soil,
come, Holy Spirit,
nourish us
in all things good
and virtuous.

As fire,
let the Spirit burn
within our hearts
until we yearn
to join the conflagration of
Christ's total,
all-consuming love.

SPARK #13
UNEXPECTED HEALING

In the early 1970s, my wife and I purchased ten remote wooded acres of land in western Massachusetts. By 1978, using our vacation time to work on the property, we were well on our way to fun and freedom, singing songs around night bonfires, and enjoying blueberries all season.

Until we acquired this property, my wife and I had always made our home in a parsonage owned by the church I was serving. Now this cabin in the woods became our home away from home. We owned it, could do as we pleased to it, change it as we desired—no committees involved, no permission required.

This property was located at the top of a mountain called Jacob's Ladder, near a summer dance theater that bore the appropriate name of Jacob's Pillow. That name referenced both the scriptural story of Jacob, the mountain on which it was located, and the mammoth boulder in its front yard. In keeping with the Biblical character identified by the name Jacob, we named our place Jacob's Rest. It was, after all, a place where I could rest from pastoral duties, pound a nail into a board, install a water heater, put up wallboard, or install a light switch without the need to redo it every week or two. Sermon writing and committee meetings never stayed nailed down for more than a week at a time.

The area was inaccessible in winter or spring except by foot, snowmobile, or tractor. However, all summer and fall, our car could safely travel the two-mile road of gravel and mud that led up to our property.

Even though Jacob's Rest was only an hour's drive from our church home, it was another world to us. Our family enjoyed our time together in our "wilderness" with turkeys, deer, muskrats, beavers, raccoons, and wildcats, not to mention snakes, field mice, and six-inch-long black lizards with bright yellow spots that lived under old, rotting logs.

This particular year, when we arrived to open up Jacob's Rest for the summer season, there awaited us a long-anticipated addition to our kitchen: a used electric stove that we had purchased at the end of the previous summer. I had installed it on a weekend visit to the cabin in late fall. Now that the stove was in place, we anticipated the wonderful luxury of instant heat, of turning on a burner rather than building a fire. This would even provide us with an oven in which to bake a blueberry pie or roast a turkey. With all the blueberry bushes in our front yard, I was looking forward to a homemade, hot blueberry pie, fresh from our newly installed oven.

But when we arrived, I discovered that, on recollection, I had questions about the electrical work I had done the previous fall. Would the stove work? To which circuit breaker in the basement had I hooked it? Had mice chewed through any wires during the winter months? These seemingly simple questions led me to ask my seven-year-old daughter to do me a service. I asked her to stand by the stove while I went to the basement to check things out and to turn on the electricity. I would shout up to her that the electricity was on, and she could tell me whether the stove was working.

The instructions I had given her were not nearly detailed enough for a seven-year-old. While I had assumed that she would tell me if any stove lights came on when I turned on the electricity or if the second hand of the clock started to move, she reasoned that the way to tell if the stove was on was to feel the heat. So, when I shouted up to her from the basement that the electricity was on, she put her right hand down on a burner that was, indeed, working and had quickly turned red-hot.

With a cry of shuddering pain, she leaped away from the stove and held out her hand to her mother, revealing the circles of blisters already forming on her small palm and fingers, mimicking the burner's shape and size. Hearing her cry, I rushed up from the basement to stand helpless and guilty before her agony.

Her burned hand looked frighteningly ugly, as if she would have pain for a long while and scars forever. The hospital was at least a half hour away, and the prospect of her hurting all that time without help was like a dagger in my heart. So, once again, I learned that when all else fails, pray; when you feel totally helpless, pray; when someone you love is in searing pain, pray; when someone else is hurting because of your error, pray; when your wife asks you to pray, pray.

So I prayed, earnestly, urgently, humbly—prayed not as a pastor of his sheep, but as a father for his daughter: "Jesus, my little girl is hurting. She was only doing what I asked her to do. It is the desire of my heart that you would heal her hand, now, fully and completely, no scarring, no pain. I confess that she is suffering due to my carelessness. Forgive me for my thoughtlessness and heal her hand, Lord, and deliver her from her pain." So went my prayer, or something very like that.

Yet, even as I prayed for my daughter's healing, there was another layer of thoughts going on at a deep level inside me, questioning my prayer. Those questions went something like this: *Will God heal this wound simply because I ask? Can God actually heal such a burn quickly or completely? Will I look silly praying for such a healing? If I pray and God does not heal, what will my daughter think, of me or of prayer? Do I have any right to pray such a prayer? Will I be raising false hopes?*

These and other negative thoughts and unhappy questions ran like a dark undercurrent beneath my praying. They smothered my faith and choked my words. But need and compassion overrode my doubts, and I staggered on. As I prayed aloud for my daughter's healing, I also prayed an unspoken prayer that God would not hold my unbelief against her, an unbelief that seemed stronger than my believing. I concluded my prayer with the hope that God would answer my prayer, but without any conviction that healing would happen.

Then, as we headed toward the car for the trip to the hospital, my daughter stopped crying, saying that the pain was going away. She held out her hand, and the blisters and silver burn marks on her palm and fingers were disappearing. *Maybe the burn was not been as bad as it first appeared,* I thought. Soon, within a minute or two, her hand was as normal as it had been before she touched the stove. There were one or two little silver traces to remind us of the burn, but nothing more. What a relief! What a miracle! What a strange coincidence, that I had prayed to Jesus just as her hand was suddenly and strangely better. So, we did not go to the hospital. Her hand had healed.

To this day, it is hard for me to acknowledge that Jesus actually healed her hand, even though I know he did. I saw the burns; I saw her pain; I heard her cries; yet her hand was made perfect in a few moments. Today, her hand is still perfect. So, in spite of doubts that gather around the facts, I choose to affirm what I know by faith and experience.

When I am asked if I believe that God can heal, I answer with a firmer "Yes" because her hand was healed. When I am asked to pray for a person to be healed, I pray more earnestly and with greater conviction because her hand was healed. I pray more fervently, not because I know God will do it, but because I know God can do it. It is not my expertise or training or proper use of words or depth of my conviction that heals. It is Jesus. So, doubts or no doubts, I pray.

Some years later, in a group meeting at the home of one of my parishioners, the host, who owned an automobile repair shop, asked me to pray for a healing in his back. He was scheduled for an operation the next day to attempt to fix a problem that was causing him extreme pain and could possibly force him to give up his business. He sat on a chair as the group gathered around him, placing hands on him while I prayed. As soon as the prayer was finished, he announced that he could feel himself being healed. He stood up, smiled a great smile, and declared his back pain gone.

The next day a preoperative x-ray revealed to the doctors that they had misread some previous x-rays, that a mistake had been made, and that he would not need the operation after all. What a coincidence. We prayed, and the doctors made a mistake.

REFLECTIONS ON "UNEXPECTED HEALING"

The truth is, I am always surprised by faith healing, just as I was when my daughter's hand was healed. But then, I'm always surprised when miracles happen, which they often do. I believe surprise is a proper response. I should be surprised. It is God's grace at work. That is always a gift, and gifts cannot be expected. Faith and doubt may learn how to live together, but faith will always be surprising doubt with gifts of grace.

It seems like doubts are always present where faith is at work. I would have questioned Moses had I been there as he called his people to set out for the Promised Land. Trust is a necessary part of believing. Doubt may be present, but faith is in charge. Such was my frame of mind when I wrote the following.

GOD, YOU'VE GOT TO BE KIDDING!

Follow that cloud?
God, you've got to be kidding.
A cloud cannot speak
or give voice to its bidding.
A cloud is no more
than a fog in the sky.
How can you imply
that it knows more than I?
When night comes upon us,
the heavens turn dark.
In blackness, we're sure
to lose sight of that mark.
Clouds have a habit
of changing their shape.
How in the world
can they help us escape?
How can we tell
which cloud is assigned us?
Will size or shape do it?
Just what will remind us?
One cloud, filled with brightness?
Yes, that would be dandy.
A fire-like lightness—
yes, that would prove handy.
We'll need such a compass
or surely we'll stray,
and the desert will kill us
as we lose our way.
Can we follow a cloud?
It seems that we must,
or stay here and die.

Guess we'll just have to trust
your spirit to show us
in vapor and fog
what doubting hides from
the will of our God.

SPARK #14

A "CONNECTICUT YANKEE ANSWER"

As I write about events that took place at Jacob's Rest, I am reminded of a neighbor who lived next door to us, a neighbor who became a shower of sparks for me. This man and his wife had been members of the church I was serving when I bought the Jacob's Rest property. They had heard about our new property, traveled north to see it, and been positively impressed. So impressed, in fact, that they bought a parcel of land right next door to us. In this case, "next door" meant about a quarter of a mile down the dirt road from our place.

We were good New England Yankee neighbors, tending to our own business, respecting each other's boundaries, both physical and personal, always willing to lend a hand when and where it might be needed. I seemed to need his help far more than he needed mine.

He was building his own house as I was building mine, and he knew what he was doing better than I knew what I was doing. As he was retired, his work went faster, looked better, and seemed more substantial. That is not to say my work was not okay. It was. But it was not of the caliber of his work, and my carpentry expertise was a mile short of his. So I lived in the glowing example of his work, my efforts overshadowed by his efforts.

I do not mean to imply in any way that he demeaned me. Quite the contrary. He was always positive and appreciative of what I was accomplishing. These uncomplimentary comparisons were taking place in my head (pride), not in his attitude. I had a harder time visiting his work than he had visiting mine.

This man was a living definition of what it meant to be a "Connecticut Yankee," even though his new property was in Massachusetts. He would "wear it out, use it up, make it do." His tools were always sharp and his planning frugal and precise. He got the job done with clever invention married to strong resolve. He was nonconfrontational with his strong opinions, and he would share them only if asked to do so. He believed in a strict honesty that bore no room for lies. One time, when a local lumberyard was not honest with him, he gave up trading with them even though they were the closest and cheapest place for him to get his lumber. If he could not trust them, he would not deal with them.

Once, he told me a story about building a chimney for a man who was always late in paying his bills, using other people's money to his own advantage. "I built him his chimney," he said, "and told him it wouldn't work unless and until he paid me what he owed me. He did not pay me, and when he tried to use the fireplace, it smoked him out of his living room. When the smoke cleared, he looked up the chimney and could see it was clear and proper. So he paid me for the work. Only then did I drop a brick down the chimney to break the sheet of glass I had built into the chimney about halfway down." That was his story, and I have no reason to disbelieve it.

Well, one day I needed his advice and help on a job I was doing at Jacob's Rest. I had just had a well drilled on my property. It was about forty feet down to the water and another thirty feet to the bottom, seventy feet deep altogether. My follow-up job was to put a submersible pump down the well to push the water up into our house. Although I had all the necessary parts and piping, I was not quite certain about how to go about doing the job. So, our phone line having been newly installed, I called my neighbor for help. His truck pulled into the yard about twenty minutes later.

We stood together in thought, looking at the parts and piping strewn about on the ground, waiting. I asked him, "How do I go about putting this pump into the well? What is the easiest way?"

His answer was a perfect Yankeeism. He said, "I don't know how you would do it, but I'll be glad to tell you how I would do it if I was doing it." Which he then went on to explain. I accepted his advice, and the job got done, efficiently, easily, and properly.

His response to my request was not simply his way of playing with words or trying to be cute or clever. Such motives did not match who he was. Rather, his response mirrored his way of living. He would not think of telling me how to do my work or live my life. He respected my freedom and his own too much for that. He was, however, very willing to share his view, his way, and his insight with me. Then I could decide to trust his way or stay with my own, choose his advice or keep to my own, knowing that he would think none the less of me however I choose.

That strange and unexpected Yankee-like response to my request was a bright shower of sparks that continues to remind me of the need to respect the freedom of every other person.

REFLECTIONS ON "A 'CONNECTICUT YANKEE ANSWER'"

When I wanted to get water from my well, I knew I needed help. I knew that if I wanted the job done right, I'd better listen to someone who knew more than I did about it. Humiliating, but necessary. So I put myself in what was, to me, the lower position of a needy person asking for help. In that position, my pride got in the way. To me, in my need, my neighbor's response could have seemed harsh, distant, rude, arrogant, a put-down and an insult. Knowing him, it seemed anything but.

Thank God for the shower of sparks that came to show me how foolish I look when I get all cramped up in my insecurities. It glowed so brightly that appreciation overcame pride and I began to understand where my neighbor was coming from. He was not degrading me. He was honoring both my freedom and my choice. His response was, in fact, loving and encouraging and nondemeaning. He did not assume a higher place.

Only when I had come to that insight did I also see the fire from which that spark had flown. Why had so simple a response affected me so deeply? The answer presented itself when I was able to connect my neighbor's response to the way Jesus often speaks to me when I call to him for help. Jesus always respects my freedom. I can accept his advice, his warnings, his way of doing things, or I can choose my own. The choice is always mine to make. Jesus seems to say to me, "I don't know how you will choose to do it, but I'll share with you how I would do it. I leave it up to you to make up your own mind. I'll love you no matter what you choose."

Thinking about how Jesus, in love, respects my freedom also helps me see how he, in response to his Father's leading, moved through life, by his choice freely offering us his life.

THE NARROW DOWN

His life reveals a narrow way
from which his footsteps never stray
or turn aside to better gain
some easy exit from life's pain.
He lets no intervening view
distract from tasks he's asked to do.

His path does not avoid the proof
that names the lie and honors truth.
The walk his Father has begun
his willing feet do not outrun,
nor does he seek for safety's sake
more than the next step he should take.
When his way leads down to less,
he walks on in his faithfulness
as in obedience he pursues his
way just as his Father chooses.
This narrow path my soul would try,
to face the hurt, to voice the cry,
to stay the pain, to touch the need,
to walk love's walk,
if need be, bleed,
to speak the truth, to name the lie,
to choose a cross on which to die,
to set my compass by his chart.

I find it very hard to start.

Narrow's harder. Wide and free
are what appeals to folk like me.
Down is narrow; up is wide.
Width and height are on my side.
Somewhere inside me, I believe
that traveling upward will achieve
true satisfaction. Paths descending
only lead to some bad ending.
Paths that lead most broadly up
are guaranteed to fill my cup.
My upward-mobile self embraces
famous names and higher places.

Yet he who leads does not agree,
the "narrow down" his choice for me.
I need the cross to gain the crown;
my way to *up* is narrow down.
With him, both life and peace are found
with those who choose this narrow down.
His down will lead me, soon or late,
in freedom, up to heaven's gate.

SPARK #15

AN ANGEL IN THE RAFTERS

I believe in angels. I guess I always have. I have had confirmation of their presence more than once throughout my life. Then, one morning in the early 1990s, on a communion Sunday, I finally saw one! It came about in this way. I had offered the communion cup to the congregation. As deacons passed trays of individual cups of grape juice and wine to the people in the pews, I was seated in the front of the sanctuary, facing the congregation, praying for those who were present.

In a most incredible and powerful way, I suddenly became aware of the Spirit of God moving in our midst. It was so strong a feeling that I looked up, as if bidden to do so by the power of the Spirit. In that sacred moment, I was given to see, almost level with the giant beams that filled the whole expanse spanning the vaulted ceiling and across the sanctuary from wall to wall, the majestic presence of a glorious angel, wings outspread, covering the congregation with a sheltering cover of calm and peace, holiness and glory.

Just here, I want to be as honest as I can about my reaction to this rather wondrous and supernatural event. I was not surprised or frightened or even incredulous. Although, in reflection, that calm and accepting response seems most unlikely, it seemed very natural at the time. I was, however, curious. Why was the angel not up front, where the communion table was? As soon as I had asked this question in my mind, I received an answer. "The angel you are seeing is the angel of this church, and the church is the people, not the building."

While I watched, I noticed what I took to be feathers falling from the outstretched wings of the angel onto the people in the pews. My curiosity being greater than my common sense, and my thoughts going where they would, I asked the Spirit, "What's wrong with the angel that it is losing its feathers?"

"Those are not feathers," the Spirit replied. "That is the love and grace of God falling upon the people."

Now, right here I really showed my theological ignorance and lack of understanding, for I quickly responded by questioning the truthfulness of the Spirit. "How can that be?" I boldly asked. "I know most of these people. Some of them are not very good Christians. Some are not even very nice people. How can your love and grace be falling on them?" This question came from the very core of my being. It erupted from my deepest prejudices. It exposed naked judgments that I had covered over with unabsorbed theological theory.

The Spirit answered with tolerable goodwill. "God's love and grace are not given on the basis of merit. They are given on the basis of need and forgiveness. Who needs God love more than those who do not know the power of it? Who receives communion here?" the Spirit asked in a seeming shift of topic.

"All who wish to receive it," I replied.

The Spirit continued with my short lesson in forgiving love. "Is not communion the sign and seal of the grace and love of God expressed in the gift of God's Son, Jesus? Is not the outpouring of his life's blood for all who will receive it? Is he not offering it to all?"

My answer was a quiet and humble "Yes."

"Then believe what you do here in communion," the Spirit admonished me.

With that, the spirit retreated, the angel vanished from my sight, and I was left alone in the front of our congregation with a vision to share and a confession to make.

I stood and shared with those present all that I had seen and heard and learned concerning the angel. To my astonishment, the congregation heard my story gladly, and I was not thereby branded a fanatic or religious nut. Indeed, most of them had sensed the power of the spirit's presence during that event, and many knew that something important was happening just by watching me. For the most part, they were glad to know that our church had an angel that was watching over them and that the love and grace of God fell on all of them, no matter. Although no one was converted that day, many had their faith deepened to new levels of commitment. I certainly did.

REFLECTIONS ON "AN ANGEL IN THE RAFTERS"

I have often wondered why I was granted the grace to see an angel. I did not seek after such a vision or secretly long for one. I'm not sure I even believed that anyone could actually see an angel in this day and age. The answer I have come to is that, like the grace and love of God, it was not given to me because of anything I was or did. It has always been clear to me that I did not deserve such a vision. Far from it. It was granted to me because I needed that encounter to deepen my faith and uncover my judgmental nature. More than that, I was not and am not the center of the story. If anything, I am the guilty party in the story. The story is about the church. The church needed to know, more than I knew or was able to teach them, how much God loved them and how freely the grace of God was being poured out upon them in abundance, and about how richly the communion of Jesus was with them, each and every one. The angel of the church made sure they got the message. I was not even the messenger. I was simply part of the message.

When I retired from that church, I gave to the congregation a pair of small angelic statues to remind them of all that God had revealed to us that communion Sunday.

A LITTLE SONG OF PRAISE

Eternal God,
beginning, ending,
Glorious God,
your angels sending,
Nurturing God,
to our needs bending,
All praises be,
O God, to thee.

Forgiving God,
your grace commending,
Shepherd God,
your sheep attending,
Healer God,
the broken mending,
All praises be,
O God, to thee.

Incarnate God,
to us descending,
Seeker God,
the lost befriending,
Protector God,

the weak defending,
All praises be,
O God, to thee.

Gracious God,
our good intending,
Mercy, love,
and justice blending,
to you, in prayer,
our thanks ascending,
All praises be,
O God, to thee.

SPARK #16
LOST AND FOUND

Being lost is one thing; knowing we are lost is another. Admitting we are lost is a third. Willingness to be found is yet a fourth. Being lost is complicated. Being lost can be both frightening and challenging. Being lost can become a test of resources, courage, and skill sets. Being lost can be a very lonely condition. So it was for me when I was seven years old and lost.

Our father had tickets to the circus. It was the world-famous Barnum and Bailey Circus, and it was in our area for a week. My older sister and I were excited beyond words. We seldom went places with our father, and this was an exceptional place to be going. We rarely had a whole day with him, and this would encompass the full day. We had never been to a circus before, and this was the very best circus a kid could ever be going to. It was a very special treat for the whole family. What could go wrong?

The circus was being staged at the armory in our city. To house a circus, the building needed to be very large. It was. As we entered the impressive and spacious entrance area, we seemed to be swallowed up in people, activities, and confusion. With all the excitement, it was not long before I needed a bathroom.

My father found out where the men's bathroom was located, and off we set through the crowds and the confusion. When we arrived, Dad told me to go in and tend to my business and said he would wait for me right at the door where we were standing.

So, somewhat proud that he was trusting me to go by myself and somewhat scared that he was sending me off by myself, I entered the men's room and did my business. That part went just fine, but in my effort to return to the place where my father waited for me, I lost my way, there being more than one door to the facility. I chose to leave by the wrong door, turned the wrong way, and was immediately lost.

At first, I did not panic. I did wonder where my father had gone. Had he left me to find my own way back to our seats? Was I on my own? Had I been deserted? What should I do next? Unsure of myself and of my father, I headed out into the stream of activities to discover where I was and where my father was. As I walked, I passed cages of circus animals—monkeys, lions, tigers, and the like. All around me, busy people were performing tasks like washing elephants, feeding horses, and cleaning up after one kind of animal or another. I felt small, vulnerable, dispensable, and out of place.

As time passed, I became more focused on my surroundings, on the activities of the circus, than on my being lost. What was going on all around me became of more interest than finding out where I was or where my family was.

But underneath it all, I was scared and ashamed. It was a strange and unwelcome situation in which I found myself. Although I made a great effort to appear normal and in control, I was terrified. Although I tried to be brave and courageous, I was anxious and ashamed. Although I appeared calm, I was trembling. Being lost became a place of unpleasant thoughts and unwelcome feelings, and I longed to be found.

Then, as if by magic, there was my father, standing right where I had left him, waiting for me where he had promised me he would. Somehow, I had come back to the door where he was standing. I had found him. He had waited for me to find him. I was safe again, whole again, embraced again, belonging again.

The circus was all I expected it to be. The day was memorable in many ways, but especially because, having been lost, I was found.

As an adult, I experienced being lost in a different way. I had been visiting a neighbor's home near our cabin in the woods. We had built a summer home on eleven acres, and the neighbors had built their home on nine acres. Between our homes, there were fourteen acres of woodland. I had decided to walk home from their home to our home through the woods. It seems an easy walk. It was not. As soon as I was out of sight of the neighbors' house, I was lost. All sense of direction seemed to evade me. Nothing in the woods looked familiar to me. No direction seemed right. If I walked the wrong way, I could well be walking all day and all night in the vast expanse of mountain forest of which our acres were part. I would run out of sunlight, food, water, and warmth. I would be helpless and exposed to the elements. What to do next? How to find my way?

Then, clearing my mind of all the thoughts that were troubling me, I simply turned to what I already knew and what I had to work with. My home was north of my neighbors' house. It was afternoon, and the sun was still high in the west. If I kept walking, keeping the sun on my left, I would, sooner or later, come to my house. It was a simple plan that worked just as I hoped it would.

When, at last, I came out of the wood and found myself directly behind our house, I experienced a sense of relief that was tremendous. I was safe again. I knew where I was. I was back in control. I was found.

Being lost happens in many ways and for many reasons. I became lost in the midst of the exciting setting of a circus because I did not know where I was in relation to my father. Again, I felt lost when, in a beautiful wood, I did not know my way home.

A third experience of being lost happened in England during my air force enlistment. This time, I felt lost because I was all on my own, trying to remain hidden while traveling in a hostile environment. It happened this way.

As a member of a flight crew, I took part in a four-day escape and evasion exercise conducted by the United States Air Force, the Royal Air Force, and the English government. It included the general population in that part of England. They were alerted to turn us in, just as they would be asked to do if they were at war and we were the enemy. It was a test for us all.

If we were shot down over enemy territory, this exercise would give us a helpful experience in escaping and evading. In fact, this was very likely to happen should we go to war. Our standing mission in war was a bombing mission from England to Russia, from which we would not be returning due to the distances involved, the fuel we could carry, and the A-bomb blast that would undoubtedly ruin our aircraft.

During this exercise, we were taken a long distance out into the countryside in closed trucks to unspecified locations far from our home base. We were given a specific point to head for. We were dressed as we would be dressed for a flight. We had no means of communication other than our ingenuity.

It was a cold, rainy, and windy day when we set out—typical English weather, inhospitable. It stayed that way for four days. I started out with a partner, a guy I did not know. He lasted about six hours. He gave himself up at a bridge because of the stream he would not cross. We had been walking through hedgerows and hay fields and thick scrub all afternoon, and he was plainly tired. He just ran out of energy. The water was the last straw. He chose to quit. It was his choice, but his choice left me without company and on my own.

While it was easier to travel without having to wait for someone or to keep encouraging someone or to give someone physical support, it was harder without a companion for company. I was soon lost in myself. Everything outside of me pushed me into myself. There were hostile weather, a hostile population, a hostile landscape, and hostile prospects. My sense of being lost included sleeping under a haystack, where I feared being punctured by a pitchfork. I also worried about drowning while crossing one of the many streams, getting hypothermia, or being captured and jailed.

I walked several miles, crossed several streams, pushed through numerous hedgerows, and had done very well in spite of fear, hunger, sore feet, and chills. Still, I was lost. I did not know where I was or whether I was going in the correct direction, or where I would end up. If that describes being lost, I was lost.

Being found did not mean just being located by others, even though that is what finally happened. On the fourth morning, a local resident spotted me and reported me to the authorities, and they captured me. I was taken to a jail where other participants were also being held. My clothes were taken from me, and I was placed in a cement cell, soaked with a firehose, and left alone, doubled over and shivering in the wet and cold. After a few hours, I was put into a room with other "prisoners." After that, the exercise was over, and we were all returned to our base.

In this case, being lost was a matter of being forced to become dependent upon myself alone. It was a matter of withdrawing into myself because of what was going on around me. It was a matter of reducing myself to as small and unresponsive and isolated a being as possible. *Lost* became simply putting one foot in front of the other, one thought in front of the other, one river and bridge after the next, one hedgerow and cold night after the next, avoiding one group of civilians after the other. In this case, discomfort was the price of survival.

REFLECTIONS ON "LOST AND FOUND"

Sacred scripture often describes folk as lost and needing to be found. As I have reflected on these obvious times when I have been lost, I have become more aware of how often and in how many ways I am lost.

I can become lost in myself—I was lost in thought. I can become lost from someone else—I lost contact. I can become lost to another—I lost track. I can become lost in some distraction—I lost interest. I can become lost in something outside of me—I got lost in my work. I can become lost in my emotions—I lost my temper. I can be lost in my intentions—I lost my concentration. In each of these situations, I need to be found, yet may not realize it or be ready to admit I am lost. In addition, I may not have any desire to be found.

I will be more readily willing to acknowledge my being lost because of the insight my reflections on being lost have given me. In the past, I recognized that I had been lost only three or four times. Now I see what scripture has always knows: that I become lost on a regular basis. On a regular basis, therefore, I need to be found and brought back to myself, to be redirected in the proper direction, to take stock of where I am and where I am heading, and to ask for directions or take advice.

Being lost may not always cause me to suffer from disorientation, produce a sense of loneliness, or cause a fear-provoking unease, but that doesn't mean I'm not lost.

LOST AND FOUND

Lost, more times then I know,
lost from the people I love,
lost to my hopes here below,
lost to the joys from above.
I'm stumbling along
in desperate despair,
unsure of what to do,
or who I am, or where.

I can get confused and stray,
get myself turned around.
Sometimes I just can't find my way.
Sometimes I must be found.

SPARK #17

WRONG AGAIN

There have been times in my life when I have had good reason to be angry, to feel hostility, to be, shall I say, less than forgiving. One such occasion happened when, while she was just out of high school, our youngest daughter became pregnant. That good news came to me at our cabin in the woods. Both daughters brought the news to my wife and me. Time has proven it to be wonderful news, but I received it without joy. It crushed me with fears and tensions. How might this undercut my ministry? How could so young a girl raise an infant baby as it should be raised? How would the baby be adversely affected by it all? As far as I was concerned, adoption seemed like the best option, and that was what was finally chosen, although my pregnant daughter seemed to have the least to say about it and the baby's father was remote and uninterested.

A Christian family, chosen by an agency, offered to have our daughter live with them until such time as a decision could be made concerning the baby. This family lived one hundred miles from us. Our daughter lived with that family during the latter part of her pregnancy. Under the pressure of such a situation, our daughter finally decided to allow the family she was living with to adopt her baby. The adopting family loved my daughter and allowed her to stay in touch with them. Her relationship with them was distant but helpful.

Much later, we were going on a trip to visit the baby, now a full-grown person and a wonderfully successful adult. There was some concern about how I would behave. When asked, I replied that I was okay with the meeting but I was still angry with the father. I said I would forgive him if and when he said he was sorry for the way he had treated our daughter and us.

In response to my answer, my daughters, in unison, confronted me with my pride, anger, and desire for vengeance. My wife joined them, and it was three against one. I was totally in the minority. The message delivered to me with force was that I was wrong in my attitude, that what I had said meant I would forgive only *if* or *when*. The *if* and the *when* were personal conditions. Those conditions insisted on my getting what I wanted before I would consider forgiving. Did I not realize how much I also needed forgiveness? Did I not understand how unlike God I was behaving?

What I had taught my daughters I now had to learn for myself. This was another painful space where I discovered I was wrong, where I found out how needy and demanding I was, where life gave me a raw edge to chew on, to consider and repent my own actions and my own need to change. My family, in love, gave me that uncomfortable space—that prized but difficult place where I could choose to grow a bit or just continue to feel angry. I have chosen to forgive, even though I have not been asked to do so by the offending party.

Another occasion for that kind of lesson happened at a parishioner's home, at the dinner table. Eight guests had gathered for "Dinner for Eight." It was a program where people shared an evening together around a meal. At the table, while eating, in the midst of the general conversation, I told a story about a gay person in a bar. The story was not humorous, but of far more importance, it was totally inappropriate for two reasons beyond the obvious. The first reason was that the host family had a gay son who had only recently come out in terms of his sexual identity. The "joke"

I told was full of uncomplimentary and untrue stereotypes. Being their pastor, I knew all about their son, and I loved him for who he was. But in one thoughtless moment, I could undo the trust they had in my relationship with him.

The second reason was very much like the first. Our well-accepted organist was gay, and his partner was a church member. What a way to dishonor both of them. Beyond the "joke" itself being wrong, it was my insensitivity that could ruin the evening, to say nothing of many treasured relationships. As a pastor, I was aiding the enemy.

As I was halfway through telling the "joke," the person sitting next to me gave me an elbow in the side and a signal with his face that said, "Shut up." Once again, I entered a space where I could choose to face my insensitivity or simply be embarrassed by it. I shut up. Later, I wrote a long letter of apology to, shall I say, the host and hostess. I apologized to the other guests. I did not try to excuse myself or explain myself. I said I was sorry because I was just plain wrong, not only for the "joke" itself but, more importantly, for that part of me that could be so thoughtless. In that unwelcome space, I learned something about myself I would not have believed if simply told I might be that way.

Yet another example of those places and spaces where difficult lessons happen was afforded to me one summer at our grandparents' farm. I was about eleven or twelve years old and was sneaking out of the house to meet a friend to do a powwow around a bonfire. The "bonfire" was in a tin coffee can filled with sand onto which had been poured a bit of gas or kerosene or candle oil, which was then lit. It worked fine. We would put the bonfire between us, talk like we thought Native Americans would talk, dance as we thought they would dance, and generally behave in ways that mimicked what we saw of Native Americans in the movies. The fire was the center of our midnight meetings. It showered us with sparks.

Anxious to share such a good time with others, I invited my cousin to a daytime powwow behind the barn. This happened on a Sunday afternoon when the whole family was socializing on the front lawn. He seemed very interested in my preparations of sand in a coffee can, lighter fluid on the sand, and a match to light it. I was very proud of myself to be able to do all this as an expert on powwows and fire building.

The joy was short-lived. I entered a very hard space when my cousin left me behind the barn, went back to the family gathering, got his father, and brought him back to see the fire his cousin had lit behind the barn. Not good. I was fine with the whole idea of fire until an adult came into the picture. Suddenly, I felt guilty, ashamed, and totally exposed. My secret life was known. My private life was now public. My small universe of me was torn open and exposed to criticism, judgment, and correction. I had nowhere to turn. I was caught. I could continue in my own little world, or I could accept the rules of the larger community. I could continue to believe I was perfectly capable of doing whatever I wanted to do with no risk and no consequence, or I could accept my responsibility in a family larger than myself, where my behavior affected others' and theirs affected me. The truth of this lesson escaped me at that moment, what with my being consumed with anger at my cousin for telling his father about me. It was hard for me to digest the obvious reality that it was I and not my cousin who was in the wrong. Somehow, I knew that my cousin was right to report me, even though it hurt like an open wound in my self-esteem.

REFLECTIONS ON "WRONG AGAIN"

By myself, I am nobody. With others, I am one somebody among other somebodies. Relating to myself is not the same as relating to others. Recognizing who I am has to do with who I am with others. I cannot express who I am all by myself. I cannot see myself all by myself. It follows that without others, I will never see myself as others see me, and so, I will never see a need to change. The me that is revealed when I am relating to others may occasionally hurt my pride and upset my opinion of myself, but there will be little growth or change in me without those encounters. Unless I accept and endure and see what showers of sparks reveal by their bright light, unless I receive the message delivered about an "underdeveloped me" from people around me, I will simply remain as I am or become worse. Nothing in me is innately who I wish to become.

No wonder scripture speaks so positively of the need for repentance, of turning from darkness (false life) toward the light (true life), of choosing to say no to that which is self-centered and yes to that which is centered in the other, of affirming life by choosing that which enriches the lives of others.

Repentance has little to do with being wrong or feeling ashamed. Being sorry, feeling guilty, being remorseful—these are empty negatives. They do nothing but limit and cripple. Fullness of life is not something we can find or develop or discover on our own. We are not asked to do so. The usefulness of shame and remorse is located in their alerting me to some aspect of myself that needs to change. When I experience a toothache, the pain does nothing to fix the problem, but it does tell me there is a problem. It is not so much what I turn away from as what I turn toward that matters, not so much who I have been as who I am becoming that shapes my relationships, my beliefs, my values, and our personhood.

My thoughtless and rude and arrogant behavior at the dinner table did not express who I wanted to be, but it did express who I was. A poke in the side was the pain that alerted me to the problem, and my embarrassed and apologetic response was my *ouch* at the pain. Yet all of it was nothing if it did not lead me to turn toward the person I wanted to be.

While some truth may seem to belittle and accuse and blame, that is never its goal. The aim of truth is to invite us to become what it embraces, never to put down or judge, always to improve, uplift, and complete. In the same vein, repentance is never so much about being wrong, about being broken or remorseful. It is about becoming.

When my cousin confronted me with my irresponsible, barn-endangering self, a self I was quite pleased with up to that moment, I was quick to defend myself. Yet, at a more basic level, I knew I could be and wanted to be and would be better than that. It took a moment of exposure to begin the process and initiate the change. It is not the truth we are presented with but our response to it that holds the power of change.

Scripture does not give us a Jesus who is seeking for followers who are sorry they are sinners so he can correct them, clean them up, and present them to his Father as respectable members of the kingdom. He is seeking followers who are willing to be changed by being in relationship with him. He is not revealing to his followers mysterious facts that have been hidden from others. He is inviting his followers to become the persons they are created to be. I do not follow Jesus to get cleaned up and de-sinned. I follow Jesus to find out who I can become in my relationship with him.

Forgiving and being forgiven, loving and being loved, serving and being served—these are not good deeds I am to perform. They are the characteristics of the relationships that will shape me into the person I am being created to be. The events in my life where I am violating my better self are not simply times of condemnation, blame, and shame. They are, rather, invitations to turn to the one in whom I find my truest and best self. When I recognize my less-than-human self—irresponsible, thoughtless, insensitive, proud, cruel, hurtful, self-centered—I am being led toward my human self, the person Jesus sees in me and calls me to be.

Relating to me with forgiveness, love, and service, he invites me to follow him. He does not say, "Stoddard, you will never measure up to our standards." He does not say, "Stoddard, if you don't straighten up, we will not love you anymore." He does say, "Stoddard, I am the way, the truth, and the life. You know who you are. You also know who you don't want to be. But the person we made you to be you do not yet know. I am the one who is able to define that life for you. I will share that life with you as I create that life in you, the life you require to be fully human, the life with the power to restore, heal, complete, and fulfil. If that is what you desire, then follow me. Love me as I am loving you, and together we will love the world, one person, one relationship, at a time."

That is God's good news. That is the gospel.

REFLECTING ON MY REFLECTIONS

After I retired from active ministry, I took up quilting, and one of my early lessons as a quilter was about patchwork beauty: many small, unrelated patches, when connected in a larger frame, become a most beautiful mosaic. So, as I have sewn together small pieces of my life, a design appears that is more than the sum of its parts. So far, it is far more than what I planned or imagined.

Another lesson from quilting has been that errors become part of the quilt. They do not ruin it, but they do change it a bit, and they attest to its being handmade and not factory- or machine-made. Quilt-like, my errors in life, intentional or incidental, serious or slight, injurious or laughable, have become part of the overall design of who I am.

One more lesson from quilting: the finished quilt finds its value when it is given away, not when it is kept. All those little pieces of me have little value in themselves until and unless they are given away, no matter what their value to me may be.

So I offer these bits and pieces, these showers of sparks, stirred up by the fires of life and offered, errors and all, to whomever might find them helpful, instructive, or simply interesting. Glory to God.